**Praise for *The Code*:**

"*The Code* has within it a call to o ⋯ his
call that gives Tony's book its power! Here is a man who is ⋯ ol-
lowing his own open heart."

—Tej Steiner, author of *Heart Circle: How Sitting in
Circle Can Transform Your World*

"Offers a clear and concise set of instructions for how to achieve our
dreams, for ourselves and others . . . inspires us to personal and commu-
nal action for a better world."

—Louise Diamond, Ph.D., peace educator and
author of *The Courage for Peace*

"Tony Burroughs reaches out through his Code and takes the hands of all
those who long to 'live with intention.' In this way, Tony lays footprints
for earnest souls to follow. His visions, his poetry, his call to intentional
living ring with lyricism and both idealism and practicality."

—Mary Anne Radmacher, author of *Lean Forward Into Your Life*

**What the *Intenders of the Highest Good* are saying:**

"I intend to improve every day so that at the end of each week, I'm
amazed at the highest good I've created for myself and those I met. I
intend to live in gratitude for received and approaching blessings."

—Sandy, Eastern Sierra

"I intend to live my life honoring these beliefs. My intentions are to . . . Be
positive and aspiring; ask, believe, and receive; always do my best and see
the best in others; live, love, and laugh often."

—Sheri, Arizona

"I started writing down everything and, to my amazement, within a week
I actually saw everything multiplying from money to happiness to better professional aspects. Intention with gratitude is a very, very powerful
manifestation tool. And also, if you intend that you are in silence, (this
means not thinking anything) a gap, peace, bliss will come faster to you."

—Lt. Rohit Sharma, Colaba, Mumbai, India

"At the first intenders circle, Steve intended that he find a good job he likes. Two days later he was called for an interview, and he got a wonderful job!"

—Zoe, Loveland, Colorado

"I grew up poor and fight a 'deprivation mindset' because of this. Embracing The Code has completely changed my life and those of the Intender's Circle I started. My favorite aspect is that this is "for the good of all" and not for selfish reasons. I live by *The Code*."

—Louise, Cincinnati, Ohio

"I am grateful to be meeting more people involved in Intender work! The more people I meet and correspond with, the more I love to share my vision. I am grateful to open my heart and acknowledge the Oneness of all of us here on this planet."

—Pambee, Redding, CA

"I moved into a room for rent and intended that this house be mine. A few days ago, the landlord offered to sell me the house at a discounted price. I now intend that all the money and resources that are required for the ownership of this home are in my hands. I am so grateful for the manifestation of this intention."

—Alyjah, Northern Virginia

## Other books by Tony Burroughs

NON-FICTION

*The Intenders Handbook*
*The Highest Light Teachings*
*The Intention Process* (video)

FICTION

*The Intenders of the Highest Good*
*The Code—The Reunion: A Parable for Peace*

# THE CODE

## 10 Intentions
for a Better World

### TONY BURROUGHS

WEISERBOOKS
San Francisco, CA / Newburyport, MA

This edition first published in 2008 by
Red Wheel/Weiser, LLC
With offices at:
500 Third Street, Suite 230
San Francisco, CA 94107
www.redwheelweiser.com

Library of Congress Cataloging-in-Publication Data

Burroughs, Tony.
  The code : ten intentions for a better world / Tony Burroughs.
    p. cm.
  Originally published: Ashland, Or. : Pass Along Books, 2006.
  ISBN 978-1-57863-429-3 (alk. paper)
  1.  Conduct of life.  I. Title.
  BJ1581.2.B825 2008
  170'.44—dc22
                                    2007033031

Text design by duttonandsherman.com
Typeset in Berkeley Oldstyle Book
Author photograph © Pagosa Photography: pagosaphoto.com

Printed in Canada
TCP
10 9 8 7 6 5 4 3 2 1

✪ Text paper contains 100% recycled material.

# DEDICATION

*This book is dedicated to you, honorable reader, with the intention that, by using The Code, you will experience all of the joys and wonders that come when you step into your power and put the Highest Good to work in your life.*

*Here at last is a Code of Conduct that transcends all social, religious, scientific, and political beliefs while bridging the gap between the mainstream and the miraculous. After many years of working with intentionality and listening to thousands of people state their intentions in our Intenders Circles, we have taken the best of what we have heard and developed The Code. The Code is specifically designed to empower you so that you can bring fulfillment into your personal life and, at the same time, create a better world for all of us to live in.*

*To apply The Code,*
*all you have to do is say it once a day.*

## THE FIRST INTENT — SUPPORT LIFE

I refrain from opposing or harming anyone. I allow others to have their own experiences. I see life in all things and honor it as if it were my own. *I support life.*

## THE SECOND INTENT — SEEK TRUTH

I follow my inner compass and discard any beliefs that are no longer serving me. I go to the source. *I seek truth.*

## THE THIRD INTENT — SET YOUR COURSE

I begin the creative process. I give direction to my life. *I set my course.*

## THE FOURTH INTENT — SIMPLIFY

I let go so there is room for something better to come in. I intend that I am guided, guarded, protected, and lined up with the Highest Good at all times. I trust and remain open to receive from both expected and unexpected sources. *I simplify.*

## The Fifth Intent — Stay Positive

I see good, say good, and do good. I accept the gifts from all of my experiences. I am living in grace and gratitude. *I stay positive.*

## The Sixth Intent — Synchronize

After intending and surrendering, I take action by following the opportunities that are presented to me. I am in the flow where Great Mystery and Miracles abide, fulfilling my desires and doing what I came here to do. *I synchronize.*

## The Seventh Intent — Serve Others

I practice love in action. I always have enough to spare and enough to share. I am available to help those who need it. *I serve others.*

## The Eighth Intent — Shine Your Light

I am a magnificent being, awakening to my highest potential. I express myself with joy, smiling and laughing often. *I shine my light.*

## The Ninth Intent — Share Your Vision

I create my ideal world by envisioning it and telling others about it. *I share my vision.*

## The Tenth Intent — Synergize

I see Humanity as One. I enjoy gathering with lighthearted people regularly. When we come together, we set the stage for Great Oneness to reveal itself. *We synergize.*

# GRATITUDES

This book and the Intenders of the Highest Good would not exist if it weren't for Tina Stober and Lee Ching. The measure of their commitment to serving humanity is total and I honor them both for it.

I'd also like to express my heartfelt gratitude to the following friends for their part in bringing this amazing work to life: Betsy Palmer Whitney, Mark Dziatko, and Connie Ritchie, the first Intenders—no matter where we are, you're always in my heart; Debra Ward, Mark Hill, and Chris and Dian Loukas, Extenders of the Highest Good and true inspirations to everyone they touch; Allan Hardy from the Friends of CWG who helps me more than he knows; Dan Hunter and Keith Garrison from Humanity's Team—finer men I've never met; Suzanne Walker, Ron Carswell, Mauricio Santorumn, and Sandra Aaron for their generous support; Matthew Bromley, the Purple Eagle, for creating the perfect Intenders Logo; Karen Aspin, who took it all and made it even better; Pam Baugh, Christy Snuggs and Spirit St. John, Intenders Internet angels; Victoria White, August Storm, and Teresa Caprio for their expert editing advice; Brenda Knight, Jan Johnson, and all my friends at Red Wheel Weiser, book publishers of the highest integrity; Tim White and Dave Powell, my brothers from way back; and Vicki Harding for her love and so much more.

I'd also like to thank all Intenders everywhere. You are the miracle!

# CONTENTS

# Introduction

## The Madness and the Miracles

Something's up. There's an acceleration going on. Everything is changing faster than before. Even if you can't explain it, you can feel it. From one perspective, it's as if we're seeing two extremes emerge: the madness and the Miracles. The madness—you know what the madness looks like—is the chaos; the horrific headlines and the nightly news hype; the wholesale selling of sicknesses of every kind; the overloaded nervous systems; the repressed emotions; the unwillingness to see others' points of view as valid, much less valuable; the enslavement to the moneylenders who have wheedled their way, not only back onto the church steps, but, even worse, into the core of the human heart; the deceit, so blatant, among our governments and their leaders—leaders whom we once respected and trusted to care about our best interests, but who now more resemble Attila the Hun.

Indeed, humanity sits at a crossroad. Those who are choosing to remain immersed in the madness of the mainstream consensus reality appear to be going into greater states of discomfort. By holding fast to our old habits and the "time is money" mindset, we unwittingly tighten the shackles that bind us to our own stress and suffering. It's as if we possess the key to the door of our own prison cell, and yet, by refusing to acknowledge that our mainstream reality is but one reality out of an infinite number of realities that are available to us, we neglect to place the key in the lock that's right in front of us and give it a turn.

The other extreme—the Miracles—is beginning to reveal itself to anyone who is willing to let go of their attachment to the status quo and explore their highest potential. Here's just one story that happened to me as I traveled across the country over the last few years.

*I was in Mt. Shasta recently, presenting a workshop in a bookstore and showing the people there how to start an Intenders Circle. Since that area of California is so beautiful, I decided to stay on after the workshop and camp for a few days with the magnificent mountain looming before me. This happened to be during the height of tourist season, but I was fortunate to find a space in a lovely campground eight miles out of Shasta where I could pitch my tent.*

*The only problem with this particular campground was that there were no bathing facilities. In order to wash myself, I had to go down to the Sacramento River, which ran through the middle of the campground, dip a gallon jug into the water, crouch down, and* pour the water over my head—hopping, cussing, and muttering the whole time because I'm a Hawaii boy who is used to warm water and this water was ICE COLD!

One afternoon, after I'd been there for about four days, I was sitting at a picnic table with a half-dozen strangers, just socializing. I really didn't know anything about them, and they didn't know about me or that I was learning to manifest things by making intentions. The main topic of our conversation was the current heat wave that had hit northern California (this was in mid-August, and the thermometer hanging on the camp manager's office said it was 108 degrees that day). As you can imagine, everyone was sweating profusely, and with the bathing arrangements the way they were, you really didn't want to be sitting downwind of anyone. At one point, there was a lull in our conversation and I just happened to blurt out, "I intend I have a hot shower tonight and get good and clean again!"

Well, they all looked at me as if I were crazy. No more than ten minutes had gone by when, suddenly, a large deer ran through the campground. It bounded past the picnic table where we were sitting and into a clearing behind us that was surrounded by a thicket of tall bushes. As I said earlier, I'm from Hawaii, and, in case you don't know it, there aren't any deer in Hawaii. I'd never seen a real-life deer before, so I jumped up and ran to get a better look at it.

All I saw when I got there was a white tail disappearing into the thicket. The deer was gone and I was left standing in the clearing about fifteen feet away from where my new friends were sitting at the picnic table. The only other thing in the clearing was a single tree about twenty-five feet tall, and on the back side of the tree *(where you couldn't see it from the picnic table), was a broken stub of a branch. The branch was at head level and hanging on it, left there by a previous camper, was one of those black plastic solar shower bags.*

*You can imagine how much fun I had carrying that solar shower bag back to the picnic table. To make a long story short, by sunset, we all had a hot shower and my new friends weren't looking at me like I was so crazy anymore.*

One of the easiest ways to make the break from the madness and step into the Miracles is by saying The Code once a day. With a little practice, you'll see The Code begin to work on many aspects of your life at the same time. Initially, it will help you detach from the madness by learning to observe it dispassionately. You'll stop buying into all the dramas and distractions of this world and start to focus on your dreams.

That's when the Miracles come in. Indeed, from the moment we learn to hold our attention on "the end result from the beginning," we are consciously creating our world, a world where everyone is treated with respect and we are all aligned with the Highest Good.

As our manifesting skills increase and we abandon our old, previously ensconced limitations, we discover how to generate free energy, re-grow limbs, rejuvenate organs, build completely new bodies for ourselves—and that's just the beginning. The more we learn to calm our minds through daily prayer and meditation, hold steadfast and focused upon our intended outcomes, and line up with The Code, the more we come to see that everything is possible.

How The Code came to me and the things I've experienced in learning to integrate these wonderful teachings into my own life is a story unto itself. It is my heartfelt intention that the pages to follow are a lot of fun for you to read, and, at the same time, that they help you step out of the madness and into a life filled with Miracles. For me, it all started when I began setting my intentions. It began with The Intenders.

Those of us who started The Intenders of the Highest Good are as awed by what happened as anyone. From four good friends meeting once a week outside the little Hawaiian town of Pahoa, people are now gathering in Intenders Circles all across the globe to say their intentions and share gratitudes for the intentions that have manifested for them. Believe me, it wasn't something we originally set out to do. We just wanted to help each other and get the most out of our lives.

It began with Tina, Mark, Betsy, and myself; for the first six months, there were just the four of us. Then Connie came aboard and, soon after that, our friends Aaron, Karen, Lois, and Alice joined our little circle. We were nine for the next several months; then, one night, to our utter surprise, thirty-five people showed up and The Intenders began to take on a life of its own. Next, our friend Pomaika'i heard what we were doing and started a circle on the other side of the island, in Kona. Not long after that, Conrad, another friend who had been a visitor to our circle near Hilo, took it back to Petaluma, California. Although we didn't realize it at the time, *a true grassroots movement was in the making.*

In the winter of 1998, I took a trip to the mainland and ended up staying in the San Francisco Bay Area for about a year. I began giving mini-workshops and, in the process, met so many people who told me they'd used the Intention Process to manifest their dreams that I started writing down some of the things I heard. In short, I became the scribe for The Intenders, and the book you're about to read is filled with stories I've collected over the last several years.

When I arrived in California to meet with Conrad's new Intenders Circle, I had thirty-seven dollars in my pocket and no return ticket. All I had with me was an old guitar, a backpack, and my intentions. In less than a year, I'd lived for free in everything from a gorgeous home atop Mount Tamalpais to a comfortable trailer out in the desert of Oakley. The details of my adventures are woven into the pages ahead, but, suffice it to say that, by the time my friend Jennifer Olson and I drove to New Mexico to present a workshop, there were seventeen Intenders Circles in the Bay Area, and along the way, everything I needed had manifested for me.

New Mexico was a turning point for me after having lived a simple, minimalist lifestyle in Hawaii for the previous twenty-five years. Within two weeks of settling into life in Corrales on the outskirts of Albuquerque, I was living in such abundance that my biggest decision from then until I left New Mexico was whether to drive the classic Mercedes convertible or take the shiny new Ford F250 truck. I was in a relationship with one of the most beautiful women I'd ever seen; we were raising Arabian horses, traveling to Tahiti, cruising the Caribbean together, and the Intention Process was working like a charm. In Corrales, I also found the time to write a very inspiring book (*The Highest Light Teachings*) and establish one of the most powerful Intenders Circles in the country. Eventually, however, I had to leave New Mexico. Other lessons needed learning.

Since then, life's been like riding a roller coaster. I've lived like a king and, just as quickly, found myself flat broke and sleeping in my old '85 Volvo on the crowded back streets of San Diego, intending that I be left alone for the night. As I write this, I'm snowed in, but warm and toasty, in a beautiful home thirty miles outside of Denver, and the lessons just keep on coming.

One thing that's helped me immeasurably is that *I knew* from the first time I made an intention and dedicated it to the Highest Good that I was living my calling. *I knew* I was doing what I came here to do. That having been said, it's also important for you to understand that I'm definitely not a guru or saintly person. For what it's worth, I've seen very few indications that the average person in our Western culture is interested in sitting at the feet of a great spiritual master. The people I've met as I've traveled across the country want to talk with someone they can identify with—someone who is going through the same trials and challenges they are, but who is learning to stay lighthearted and uplifted regardless of what's going on around them. In fact, the message throughout this book is that we are moving into a spiritual culture and in order to do so we must let go of the mainstream reality and simply *observe* it while we happily go about our daily lives. In this way, we retain our balance and set a good example for those around us by keeping a positive outlook.

As for me, I've known for quite some time that our world is changing rapidly and that many of our conventional ways are outdated and don't serve us anymore. As I traveled across the country, I found that I wasn't the only one who realized what was going on. I began to notice a common thread running through my conversations with other Intenders, so I started keeping a list of the ideas we talked about. To name a few: we agreed that our priorities were moving from a service-to-self attitude to a service-to-others attitude; from a doubting mindset to a trusting mindset; from a harmful, violent mentality to a more caring, loving mentality; from negative thinking to positive thinking; from a focus on the collective, consensus reality to focusing on a bigger picture; from inflexibly holding onto the "old ways" to a willingness to explore the unknown; from being enamored with the world outside us to becoming more curious about what's going on inside of us; and so forth.

Clearly, the people I was meeting were looking for a way to cross the bridge between the mainstream and the miraculous.

As I became more and more excited about the content of my list, I wondered how to put these ideas together so that they'd be palatable for the average person. At about this time, some new, very unique friends came into my life.

Before I go on, you need to know that what I'm about to tell you may sound a little far-fetched. Please understand that I'm a very practical man, not prone to accepting things unless I've seen them work for myself. I probably wouldn't even have considered printing some of the ideas in this book if I thought our world was running along fine. But it's not. Indeed, it looks like we may be headed into places we really don't want to go. So if the ideas that follow seem a little unusual, please bear with me. They're meant to help you. They're offered in the spirit of Love.

The new friends I was making were not visible, at least not to the naked eye. They came to me in my mind, in dreams, and sometimes through my close worldly friends. Again, I know this sounds strange, but when you read further I don't think it will matter where I got my information, because the quality of the information speaks for itself. In other words, I'm asking you to suspend your disbelief for a short time, and bear in mind that it's not the messenger that's important. It's the message.

The first new friend I met was Lee Ching. We'd been meeting in our small original Intenders Circle for about a month when, one night, Mark mentioned that Tina had a unique gift. Right away, my ears perked up because I'd been living by myself in a small coffee shack way back in the hills of the Big Island for the past twenty-five years, and anything that didn't look like a guava tree would have caught my interest. I immediately asked Tina what Mark was talking about, and, in the conversation that followed, I found out that she had a talent that she'd never mentioned in the three years I'd known her. She acknowledged, humbly, that she'd been a "messenger" during the 1980s in Encinitas and Del Mar, California, as part of a group of people who were known back then as Love in Action. She went on to explain that they held gatherings on a regular basis, and that it was not uncommon for her to have large numbers of people come to hear her "channel" an entity she called Lee Ching. When she said that, Mark interrupted her and said that one night, while she was in a trance and Lee Ching was speaking through her to a large group of people, a man in the audience began to heckle her. Mark explained that it frightened her so much that she gave up appearing in public from then on.

To make a long story short, I blurted out, "Well, Tina, let's get Lee Ching out of the box!"—and, after a few moments hesitation, she agreed. What happened next, I could never have imagined in a million years. She closed her eyes, said a prayer, and out came the most beautiful, caring, loving Being I'd ever met.

To my utter surprise, my gentle, unassuming friend, Tina Stober, turned out to be a world-class channel. From the very beginning, I asked Lee Ching every question I could think of. This was in the mid 1990s, so I questioned him about the economy, our government's agenda, the volcano (we could see the glow from Kilauea in the sky at night), my health, my gardens, my love life. You name it, I asked him about it. Looking back on it all now, I can say, unequivocally, that he answered every question accurately and with a feeling of such Love and compassion that I never wanted our sessions together to end.

It was Lee Ching who helped us create the Intenders Circle format. When I mentioned that I thought something was missing from our meetings, he replied, "Why don't you say some of your gratitudes into the circle and see what happens?" When I said that I was interested in the properties of sound and how they affect us, he said, "Why don't you *tone* for a while after you've finished with your intentions and gratitudes?" Boy, was that a biggie! From the first time the four of us toned, it felt like our souls fused together. We experienced a Oneness.

You'll read many of the other things he taught us throughout the rest of this book, but suffice it to say that, between the five of us—Mark, Betsy, me, Tina, and Lee Ching—we developed the ideas that gave birth to The Intenders. I can't take any of the credit. I was just the scribe until . . .

One evening at Alva Kamalani's house in Hilo, with about forty Intenders in the circle, Lee Ching told me that he wasn't exclusive to Tina; that he would come through me if I asked him to. He told me to go home and do my morning meditation, and, after I was done, to say a special prayer (it's on page 21 of this book) and have a small tape recorder ready nearby.

The following morning that's exactly what I did. At first, I couldn't believe what was happening. It was weird. But, at the same time, I felt different, lighter. All sorts of interesting information, which I'll share with you later on, started coming into my head. When I announced my skepticism, he said just to keep doing it and trust that the more I practiced, the clearer I'd get.

Looking back, I can see that he was right, even though I continued to be skeptical at times. For instance, after a lively workshop at the Soul Esteem Center in St. Louis a while back, I remember asking him: "Lee Ching, how can I know this is really happening, that I'm really in touch with you and all of the other invisible beings who say they're here to help me?" His answer, put so sweetly, was: "Tony, where do you think all of the wonderful books that you're writing are coming from?"

Hmmm . . . he had me there. I had to admit that a lot of the information written in my books was totally unfamiliar to me on a conscious level. Obviously, it had to be coming from somewhere.

Needless to say, as practical as I once was, now I'm thoroughly convinced that "something" much different is going on beyond what we were taught as children. Our world is not like we thought it was. There are invisible helpers around us—all of us—and all we have to do to contact them is believe that they are there and call them forth.

In our Intenders Circles, we always asked for help from other realms. As the format for our meetings evolved, we decided to add a thirty-minute segment at the end of the evening for receiving guidance from our invisible helpers. Usually, Lee Ching came through, but there were others, including Jesus, Mary, White Buffalo Calf Woman, Melchizedek, Maitreya, and Madame Pele who also spoke to us. It was a very exciting time for us, because we never knew who was going to speak. I recall one especially interesting spiritual guidance session when Lee Ching was talking about all of the help that's available to us from invisible sources. In part, he said, *"The Native American teachers are returning. They speak to you through your reading and in the stillness of your mind. Sometimes they even speak to you through the rocks, the animals, the trees, or the wind."*

As if to confirm Lee Ching's message, soon after that I met an extremely charismatic Indian man. The first time he spoke to me, this is what he said:

*We are The Intenders Tribe and you are one of us. You were with us, ages ago, when we came together and planned The Intenders Reunion. As with the 100th Monkey Principle . . . the Godspark . . . or the tipping point, the Reunion begins when enough people have given up their old ways and opted to line themselves up with the Highest Good.*

*The last time we met, you helped us design a personal honor code that would guide your people through this time of great change*

*and prepare you for the Reunion. We call it The Code and it con-*
*tains ten principles or "Intents" that you can set.*

*Every time you set an intent, you move all of us one step closer*
*to the day of the Reunion. We have returned at this time (just as*
*you requested) to remind you of these things, so that you can get*
*ready for the upcoming festivities.*

*The Reunion is at hand. The Tribe is gathering now. A place is*
*being held in the circle for you.*

*We await your return . . ."*

These words, and the vision that accompanied them, came during the process of creative writing. I'd said my prayer and closed my eyes when, suddenly, my imagination opened up and I found myself taking a hike on a crisp, sunny morning along an old country road. Right away, a handsome Native American stepped out from the tree line and started talking to me. He said his name was Eagleheart and that he and his tribe, which he called The Intenders Tribe, had been forced, with the coming of the white man over 400 years ago, to retreat back into the safety of the forests. He said that they'd ducked back into the woods and remained hidden among the trees ever since, not wanting to associate with us after what they'd seen us do to their brothers and sisters who'd been caught out in the open. (The story of Eagleheart and The Intenders Tribe is told in it's entirety in *The Code—The Reunion: A Parable for Peace.*)

We chatted casually for a long time, and then, curiously, right in the middle of our conversation, he turned serious, looked me straight in the eye, and asked if I stood for the Highest Good. Without hesitating, I answered, "Absolutely!" His smile instantly returned and he said that it was good to meet another member of the Tribe. Then he invited me to take a walk in the woods with him to meet the rest of his friends.

From the very beginning, The Intenders Tribe treated me with the greatest respect. Their attitude toward me or the white man in general was anything but bitter. Instead, they had a gentle kindness about them and appeared to look upon humanity with a compassion like you'd have for a child who's lost his way. They sat in a circle and told me that they'd been watching the activities of our people for the last 400 years and that now, with things starting to heat up faster than ever, they had some comments they wanted to make that they thought would help us out in the days ahead.

For openers, my new friends stressed the importance of looking at the bigger picture. They said that it wasn't wise to place the blame for our challenges on anyone in particular or on humanity in general, but that, for the most part, our chaos was being caused by a band of higher, spiritual frequencies coming from out in the cosmos. They said that these energies were harbingers of a great shift that would give way to a golden age of manifestation in the near future. They also said that our scientists had been aware of these higher frequencies for a long time, but had decided to keep this information a secret from the general public until they could figure out exactly where the frequencies were coming from. According to The Intenders Tribe, these higher frequencies would wreck havoc on mankind for the next several years, causing those who weren't spiritually advanced to deal with all sorts of crazy, erratic behavior.

They told me that there is no place to escape from the effects of the higher frequencies that are bombarding the Earth at this time, and that everyone is being touched by them in one way or another. They said it may appear as if our whole way of life is collapsing, and that we're apt to see large numbers of people brace themselves for the worst. They also said that many would feel as if they were under tremendous pressure, while being simultaneously lulled into an all-pervasive attitude of indifference that would leave them immobile and thinking that nothing they could do would affect the direction their lives were taking.

Fortunately, my new friends in The Intenders Tribe said that there *is* a way out, and that we could learn to deal with the effects of these higher frequencies by becoming less dense, more spiritualized beings. That's when they gave me The Code and asked that I do my best to get it out to the world. They told me that, from the moment we started setting the First Intent, we'd no longer be as easily influenced by forces outside ourselves. Instead of feeling helpless, like those who choose to let their innate potential sit idle, we would begin to feel more alive and better able to cope with what's happening around us. Of course, obstacles and challenges would still present themselves along the way, but, with practice, we'll come into alignment with our Highest Good and be better equipped to retain our emotional equilibrium during these challenging times—and beyond.

My new friends also stressed that the more we read *The Code*, the more we'll begin to see the positive side of the chaos in the world, and the more we'll realize that our challenges are providing us with the perfect training ground for developing ourselves. In fact, they said that any adverse circumstances we may experience will actually cause us to become more interested in learning how to master the fine art of manifestation so that all good things can come to us.

## — An Intenders Story —

*While living in New Mexico, I found that I liked going out into the desert, and it was there, on a mesa near Chaco Canyon, that I made an intention to access higher knowledge. I went into a mild trance and suddenly Kokopelli, the most outrageous Being I ever met, appeared. After playing his flute and dancing around for a while, he told me that one of humanity's most fascinating traits had to do with our strange but stubborn urge to hold onto beliefs and activities that didn't serve us anymore. He placed our current collective reality in that category and made light of it, saying that these characteristics were soon to be obsolete and seen by the masses as the old ways (not to be confused with the ways of our ancient ancestors when they were in their glory). He pointed out that the abbreviation for the old ways is "OW!" and he got up and jumped around like he'd just stubbed his toe. We laughed for a long time, then he went on to say that the new evolved ways, as represented in The Code, were abbreviated "NEW!" and that they would lead us out of our current despair into a golden age.*

*"Take your pick!" he said, as he hopped around on one leg. "OW!" or "NEW!"—and each time he shouted "OW!" he exaggerated his pain even more. I'll never forget how hard we laughed. Later on, when I was confronted by a difficult situation that stemmed from me holding on too tightly to my old ways, recalling his antics that day out on the mesa somehow made it easier to deal with.*

*Tony Burroughs*
*Pagosa Springs, CO*

When The Intenders Tribe gave me The Code, it was clear right away that it came with an inherent responsibility. If my writings were going to have any credibility, I'd have to integrate the Ten Intents into my own life, even though that would require me, on occasion, to take a few more risks than I was used to taking. I've done my best to do that and, as a result, I don't work a 9-to-5 job anymore; instead, I'm intending and trusting, every step of the way, that everything I need will be there for me in the exact moment I need it. Likewise, I'm not always sure where my next meal is coming from or how my next bill is going to get paid. I used to worry a lot about these things, but I don't anymore. Most of the time, there's more than enough of everything I need.

I can't tell you that it's always been easy. It hasn't. As I said earlier, my old habits have gotten me into jams on many occasions. Sometimes, an adverse situation would arise, and I'd get angry and fly off the handle. I'd shake my fist at the sky and scream: "How can this craziness possibly be in my highest and best good?" But it was. It *was* in the Highest Good for me to have to deal with my challenges because, without them, I wouldn't have gotten stronger. Without them, I'd still be stuck on the same old merry-go-round, giving into my immoderation or stubbornness or forgetfulness.

Nowadays, I look differently upon the challenges that life sends me. Whenever I see adversity coming, I immediately return to *The Code* and read the Ten Intents. The Code has given a positive direction to my life. It and the Intention Process have taught me something I never learned in school. They have taught me *how to think*. They've made me a lot more powerful than I was before. And I'm also more at peace.

*And that's my intention for you, if it happens to be in your Highest Good.* **The next time** *you're going through a challenge—any challenge at all—pick up* The Code *and set your intent. Choose the one that's best for you and repeat it until you know it by heart. Then all you have to do is wait for life to offer you an opportunity to use it. My friends in The Intenders Tribe say that you won't have to wait long, what with the way things are speeding up lately. When you really think about it, it doesn't matter whether it takes minutes or months. What matters is that you do it, because, ultimately, by setting these intents, you'll receive one of God's greatest gifts: You'll* become empowered. And who knows, maybe somewhere along the way, you'll decide to gather together with some of your friends and combine your intentions so that you can help create a better world for all of us to live in.

Soon there will be so many new Masters
running around and touching everyone
that this world will be
a beautiful place to be,
a Heaven on Earth.
It is possible!

# THE FIRST INTENT
# SUPPORT LIFE

*I refrain from opposing or harming anyone. I allow oth-ers to have their own experiences. I see life in all things and honor it as if it were my own. I support life.*

The first time Lee Ching "came through" me, I was sit-ting in my favorite armchair, having just finished my usual morning meditation. I'd stated my intention—*that everything needing to be known is known on this day; that all of my words are clear, precise, uplifting, helpful, and fun (I added the fun part); that I am guided, guarded, and protected throughout this entire experience; and that everything I say and do serves the highest and best good of the Universe, myself, and everyone every-where*—then I switched on a portable cassette recorder and asked myself the first question on a short list that I'd prepared in advance. It had to do with mankind's highest priorities.

Following that, I closed my eyes and, much to my surprise, within seconds I began to feel a change go on inside of me. It was very subtle at first, but then, right away, a gentle warmth began to spread throughout my chest, accompanied by a feeling that could only be described as "compassion for all living things." At the same time, I felt lighter, not in the physical sense, but as if I were more radiant, more luminescent. As I held my attention on this wonderful light, it spread out in all directions from my heart, encompassing my entire body and even past the edges of my skin, so that I found myself surrounded by a "bubble" of light. (Later on, I learned how to expand this bubble considerably farther, to fill the room I was in and even past the walls of the house to the land outside and beyond.)

Meanwhile, my body began to change; my posture shifted, my facial expression was entirely different, and the movements of my hands and arms slowed down, becoming more graceful, as if they'd taken on a life of their own.

Just as soon as my body settled into its new stature, words—softer, more soothing than I'd ever heard—came into my head. Initially, I was frightened to repeat them aloud, but, because I was completely alone at the time, except for the little kitty who had settled in quietly beside me, I (he) began to speak into the tape recorder:

*"The highest priority for humanity is to support life," he said. "Your potential as human beings is far, far greater than you presently imagine. In order for you to reach the heights of experience*

*that await you, that you have set for yourself, and that call out to you even in this very moment, you must stay alive. You must act to perpetuate your own life, as well as the lives of all those with whom you share your magnificent, abundant Earth."*

My entire being tingled with excitement as he spoke. The only time I'd ever felt anything like this was once when I slipped out of my body while meditating in a bamboo forest in Kona many years before.

*"The teachings,"* he went on, *"that are coming to you at this time are meant to reveal the true nature, the true power of your thoughts to you. Each thought you entertain either takes you closer to your joy or farther from it; and it is for you to discern, in each moment, which of your thoughts are serving you, and which of your thoughts are not serving you.*

*"Since you are becoming that which you hold your attention upon, you would be wise to support life in all that you think and all that you say. Up until now, much has been hidden from mankind concerning the dynamics of your thoughts, and you have not been properly taught how to think. Now, however, these teachings are being made available to all so that you can sharpen your thinking processes and create better lives for yourselves."*

He paused for a second, and I felt the twinkling of a smile cross my face. A part of me heard the tape whirring softly and felt the cat nestled against my leg, but my primary focus remained on the warm feeling inside of me and the flow of words coming from within. There was something else going on, as well. It was as if, somehow, between the words, he was helping me untangle eons of confusion that had been passed down to me through my ancestral lineage.

*"As you truly look to support life, you will soon see that one of the most detrimental things you can do is to oppose someone else. When you oppose anyone,"* he said, *"you invite your worst fears to come alive. By taking a defensive stance against anything or anyone, you are actually creating or setting the scene for you to be attacked. It works this way: your thoughts are always creating your future. When you are opposing others, it is because you are picturing someone else doing something bad to you. This is a thought, and, like all thoughts, it is working its way into the stream of your daily experience. Whether the person you are thinking about is a grouchy neighbor, a terrorist, a soldier, or an attacker of any kind doesn't matter. What matters is that you understand that your thought of being attacked is going to manifest as quickly as any other thought. You must learn that it is you who ultimately makes the choices about which thoughts to place your attention on. It is you who invites goodness or chaos into your experience. It is you who is responsible for your creation."*

I felt his compassion for humanity and what we're going through in these turbulent times. Lee Ching had been a great warrior who, in his own time, set an example of mercy for his people by deliberately laying his sword aside during a battle and subsequently ascending. As if he knew what I was thinking, he said: *"One of the great lessons of your lives is that you attract to yourself, and must live out in your everyday experience, that which you oppose. You must learn to allow others to go through life without your interference, and know that your unwanted expe-*

*riences will cease only when you have finally relinquished your tendency to resist them. Your opposition to anything, be it a person or an institution, always makes things worse."*

We talked for about an hour and he reiterated that, in the great majority of situations, whatever is happening does not require our participation or intervention. In fact, he said, we are usually best served by retaining our composure and intending that we are guided, guarded, and protected at all times. In this way, we save our energy for when we really need it, and, at the same time, we set an example for those around us who may be prone to emotional outbursts and getting themselves into trouble. He was adamant that peace begets peace, and that those who aspire to be effective role models won't force their beliefs on others. They'll understand that the Universe is taking care of everything and that, in most instances, they don't need to do anything at all. Then, he asked me to take a look back at the grand adventure that had been my life, and he said that I'd likely surprise myself by noticing that the times when I had the most beneficial impact on things was when I stepped back and simply observed the situation.

Just before he took his leave, Lee Ching said that a second way to support life is to spend some quiet time alone every day. This idea sounded a little odd to me at first, but the more I thought about it, the more I realized that those who meditate daily are much less likely to become involved in conflicts. They're calmer, less excitable, and, even more important, they're more apt to see things from a higher perspective. Later on, he told me that this is why those who seek to manipulate us don't want us to meditate because it makes us more difficult to control. Meditators aren't as reliant upon others to tell them what to do because they're cultivating their own inner independence. Compared to most people, they're a lot freer.

I went to bed that night pondering everything Lee Ching had said. The idea of inviting an attack by taking a defensive posture intrigued me. As I thought more about it, I recalled an experience I had in Kona in the mid 1970s. The eighteen years I'd spent farming there were very enlightening for me, mostly because of a friendship I enjoyed with a man named B.J. B.J. was a strong, lanky fellow [who looked] curiously like some of the pictures I've seen of St. Germain. When I met him, he said that he'd been an instructor with a present-day, quasi-mystery school that operated out of the east San Francisco Bay Area during the sixties and early seventies called the Morehouse. The primary draw to the Morehouse, he explained, was to help people get more of whatever it was that they wanted.

Naturally, this idea sounded good to me. At the time, I had just purchased four and a half acres near the small town of Captain Cook in the heart of Kona coffee country. My property was a long thin strip at 1,700 feet elevation, running lengthwise down the mountain, with a spectacular view of the entire south Kona Coast. The only problem was that the land was so steep I couldn't take care of it by myself. I needed help if I was going to realize my dream of making the property as beautiful and productive as it could possibly be. Enter B.J.— and, as it turned out, he was skilled in just about everything I needed to know. He knew how to plant fruit trees, design rock walls and terraces, fix a truck engine, plumb a water system, build a house, you name it. In fact, he not only knew how to do these things; he was something of an expert at them. And, to my good fortune, he was willing to share his knowledge with me.

Within a few weeks of our first meeting, B.J. moved onto my property and we began working together on a daily basis. Back in those days, we'd start our mornings out with a couple cups of strong, fresh-brewed Kona coffee while he talked about a very interesting body of ideas that he called *the Information*. At first glance, the Information didn't appear to have any particular structure to it, though it was always strangely ironic that whatever problems I was faced with at any given moment seemed to lend themselves to the Information. Over the years, I came to see that it was B.J. himself who'd set up many of my challenging situations so that I could apply the Information and learn my next lesson in life. While all of this was going on, however, I was totally unaware of his behind-the-scenes involvement.

The stories of what I went through back in the hills of Kona, with no one but me and B.J. around, are too numerous to elaborate on here, although one experience which involved the Information stands out clearly in my memory because it's played such an important part in my life. It happened one morning while B.J. and I were discussing the neighborhood tyrant, Dead Doug. At the time, Dead Doug wasn't dead yet; it wasn't until later that he killed himself by overloading on drugs and missing one of the sharp curves on the narrow road that snaked its way to the southern tip of the Big Island. When he was alive, however, Dead Doug enjoyed nothing better than to terrorize everyone who lived on the bumpy thoroughfare known as Rabbit Hill Road. At least a couple of times a month, skinny little Dead Doug would get a bug in his britches and decide to walk up and down our road with his Detroit street-punk attitude hanging out. His usual tactic was to carry a big stick or a machete in his hand and threaten to "get da boys from down south" on anyone who didn't do whatever he wanted. It was an absurd situation, but very real nonetheless. We all lived in fear—except, of course, for B.J.

Before we go any further, you need to know that we treasured our privacy back in those years on the farm in Kona and did everything we could to keep ourselves free from distractions while B.J. passed the Information along to me. Our houses were neatly hidden from the road that ran through our property by a thick grove of guava and banana trees, and hardly anyone, except for our immediate neighbors, even knew we were there. The only time we ever had to deal with other people was if we invited them up, or when one of the neighbors who lived past us (this included Dead Doug) had to cross through the middle of our land in order to get to their own farms.

On the particular morning in question, Dead Doug was down on the road, yelling at the top of his lungs. We could hear him through the trees, threatening that we'd better get down the hill immediately and fill a hole in the road, or else he was going to burn our houses down. Since I'd seen this kind of thing happen before, I knew well enough to wait until he drove away before going down and throwing a few shovelfuls of dirt into the hole.

A couple of hours later, after Dead Doug had gone to town, I was fine-tuning the job with a scratch rake when B.J. walked up and motioned to a spot in the shade of my old Power Wagon where we could talk. He'd also heard Dead Doug shouting earlier and knew I was still a little rattled by it all.

The first thing he said made no sense to me at the time, considering the circumstances of the day. He said that whatever we put our attention on, that's what we can expect to see happen in real life in the near future. He said that it got especially interesting when our thoughts were about other people, and that if we found ourselves in opposition to them, we would wake up one day to find that we'd become just like them. He said he didn't think I wanted to be like Dead Doug.

It was a stretch for me to fit this into my thinking, but he went on to say that, if I paid too much attention to Dead Doug, then very soon I would find myself thinking about ways to get back at him. My thoughts would turn dark, and I would be picturing myself lighting fire to his house, or hiring some nasty Hawaiian thugs to get him before he got me. B.J. said that I had better things to think about, like how to help the fruit trees grow better, or how to stay happy. Besides, he said, the Universe had ways of taking care of people like Dead Doug that didn't require my participation.

Four months later, B.J.'s words came true when Dead Doug left the planet, and everyone on Rabbit Hill Road breathed a sigh of relief and went back to enjoying their lives in freedom and peace.

Aside from my encounters with Dead Doug, I lived simply during my years in Kona, always protecting my freedom and doing whatever was necessary to remain unencumbered by the usual fears and controls that were accepted without question by most of my fellow travelers. I'd purposely arranged my life as a hermit so I could avoid becoming entangled in the consensus reality matrix. I never dreamed that I would leave my avocado farm and meet Lee Ching a decade later. Nor did I think I would ever leave the beautiful island of Hawaii. It was my home, my land was paid for, the trees were dripping with fruit, and I could have easily lived out the rest of my life there. Ultimately, however, as The Intenders began to blossom and I began to write books, I realized that my work had to be taken out to the world.

As I said earlier, my travels first took me to the Bay Area, then to a lavish lifestyle in New Mexico, and finally to San Diego, where I became acquainted with a group of people who introduced me to yet another way to support life. As it turned out, these new friends were members of a nearby church, and I became interested in the principles they lived by. One principle of theirs, in fact, appealed to me immensely. They didn't "backbite" other people. Or, as we said in Hawaii, they didn't "talk stink" about anyone else. Previous to this, I'd occasionally find myself taking part in conversations in which people were talking about someone else who wasn't there. All too often, the tone of these talks would shift to the negative, and, when this happened, it never felt right to me. I admit that I did it, but later on, when I went home and reflected on it all, I'd realize that I was doing the very thing that I'd opposed in the person I was just "talking stink" about. I was becoming like the person I was opposing with my backbiting.

It was like a breath of fresh air being around my friends from the church, because they rarely "talked stink" about anyone. If, on occasion, they did start to gossip or "backbite" others, they'd invariably catch themselves and stop doing it. I truly admired this about them and came to understand that their abstinence from backbiting was just another way of supporting a higher quality of life for all of us.

*When we realize that we are becoming exactly like those we oppose, shouldn't that be reason enough for us to stop opposing them?*

When you really think about it, supporting life, in itself, is a strange topic to be talking about. Under normal circumstances, there'd be no need to discuss it because we'd likely agree that it's important for us to stay alive. But circumstances in today's world are far from normal. Life is not valued here on Earth as it should be. On the contrary, we glorify the harming of others while just about everyone stands back with their hands in their pockets and takes all of the suffering for granted; the only exception comes when it's our own lives that are on the line.

Clearly, we live in an insane world, and why so many support the status quo is an unfathomable mystery to all thinking, caring people. It's as if we've lost sight of our most precious commodity, *life itself*, forgetting that, unless we're willing to stand up on behalf of our own self-preservation, we run the risk of losing all that we hold near and dear.

So, let's draw a line in the sand right now. If you believe that it's all hopeless, and that there's no chance we can create a better, safer world for ourselves, then you may as well skip the First Intent and go on to something else. Perhaps you'll want to move ahead to one of the other Intents of *The Code* and work on it for awhile.

If, however, you really do have a genuine fondness for your life and the lives of all those with whom you share this beautiful Earth, then perhaps there's a way for us to get out of the mess we're in. Perhaps, together, we can put our thoughts to their best use by envisioning (and thus beginning to create) the dawning of a new day when all people are walking the Earth freely, when all children born here are assured of living out their natural lives to completion, where the elderly are loved and cared for, and where we are all being given everything that we need. *It is possible!* Now, let's take the next step by beginning to hold that vision and make it a reality.

In addition to not opposing anyone else, there are several other things we can do on behalf of the preservation of all life.

First, we can begin to think and act more globally. This means that, in our hearts and minds, we can align ourselves with humanity as a whole instead of continuing to hold onto our allegiance to any particular nationality. This shift in our basic beliefs immediately sparks us with a new outlook toward our world, so much so that if someone were to walk up and ask where we're from, we might say, "I'm from Mother Earth, and I no longer identify myself with any nation because it looks to me like that's just another way of dividing us and getting us to fight with each other. Personally, I support life. I support *everyone's* life."

Of course, this new approach is a bit frightening for some people. I've learned this because, after having posed similar ideas to the people in my workshops, many of the comments I received were the same. Here's an example of a response I commonly hear:

*"I can't really support life as much as I'd like because, if I did, I'd have to drop my allegiance to the government. That's just too scary for me right now. Please don't misunderstand. I cannot stomach all the violence, and I'm sure we can find ways to resolve our national problems without having to resort to killing one another. It's just that I'm afraid of what the government will do to me if I don't go along with them."*

If this has a familiar ring to you, there are two things you can do: first, you can *intend and trust* that you're always guided, guarded, and protected; and second, you can begin to take a deeper look into the mindset of a tyrant. Tyrants—whether they wear the mask of friend or foe—are by nature self-centered, untrustworthy, and dangerous. There is, however, an upside to having an encounter with a tyrant. When a tyrant shows up in your life, it usually means that you are being tested to see if you can stay focused on your own core values. If you can love your enemies without joining their camp; if you can learn to observe them dispassionately; if you can continue to support all of life, *including your own*, while they threaten you, then you will have passed the test.

People everywhere are beginning to realize that our nationalistic ideals will soon be obsolete, while, at the same time, our global identity is awakening. We're seeing that, when we begin to act more from a global or humanitarian standpoint, it doesn't serve us to vote, or to watch the "national" news, or to join a political party, or even to talk about politics or the national scene in casual conversation. These kinds of behaviors are born out of fear and, as such, they reinforce the collective national identity and detract from our new allegiance as global citizens. If we find that we're gravitating toward these activities more often than we'd like, we might consider asking ourselves why we'd want to spend our precious energy patching up our old way of life now that so many brighter, more promising scenarios are being made available to us.

Something else we can do to support life is to get outdoors more often. Our ancient ancestors, without exception, stressed the importance of communing with Great Nature. They said that the wisest among us always remembers to take a walk in the woods, or go to the beach or lakeside, and take it easy on a regular basis. They recommended that we take a closer look

at the beauty that surrounds us and consider that every part of
Nature is alive. They said that, if we approach it with love, it
will renew us. It will recharge us. Think about how much better you felt the last time you got away from the hustle-bustle
of the city for a while, and you'll see that this is true.

## — An Intenders Story —

*We go camping a lot and have since we were little children. Our
parents used to pack up the station wagon on Friday evenings and
drive my brothers and sisters and me out to the woods. Our favorite place was about twenty miles from town in a grove of trees
that bordered a beautiful oblong lake. There weren't many people
camping around us back then, but now, since it is so lovely, it's
packed all weekend long.*

*In the old days, we used to hunt in the nearby woods. We didn't
see how special it was, so we'd kill all kinds of animals, chop the
trees and bushes indiscriminately, dump stuff in the water, and
leave a big mess behind when we went home. It didn't matter to us
back then.*

*Somewhere along the line, though, we made a conscious inten-
tion to remember just how sacred it was to be out in Nature. I don't
remember exactly how it came about, but, over time, we gained
an appreciation for the lake and the forest that we didn't have
before. We slowed our pace down and began to approach our time
in Nature more lightly, more gently. We started cleaning up after
ourselves so you couldn't tell we'd been there. And we stopped killing the animals. If, by accident, we harmed an animal or a plant,*

*we did as the Native Americans did—and we thanked it for its gift to us.*

*That's when we noticed the change. It started to feel better out by the lake. Animals that used to run and hide when we were around began coming right up to us. Any firewood that we needed was always nearby. And, beyond all of that, a feeling of peace is there now that wasn't there before. Even though we have a lot more activity around us, our little campsite is so peaceful that other campers always stop by and remark about it.*

*All said and done, we have a much better time out by the lake now that we take care of it, instead of harming it. And sometimes late at night, when I lie in my sleeping bag and look up at the stars, I feel so good I never want to leave.*

*Ramona Miramontes*
*Tempe, AZ*

It's time for those of us who really want to make a difference to take heart amid all of the chaos that surrounds us and begin to create a better world, without expressing our anger, without fighting or opposing anyone. We need to hold our focus on the good in the world and trust that it will multiply just because we *intend* it. As we begin to honor and support all of life, others will see our example and discover the wisdom in it. They, in turn, will take heart and begin to follow our lead by envisioning peace and holding that vision until it's a reality. Then, as we imagine everyone—from the leaders who presently seem hell-bent on destroying everything, to the unhappy neighbor who threatens our well-being—withdrawing their swords, setting their anger aside, and allowing others their due respect, we will surely create, now and forevermore, a world where each and every one of us is living in peace and comfort, with laughter and grace, in freedom and joy, aligned with the Highest Good, and touched by the heart of God.

Support Life means
we nourish,
we feed instead of foul,
we care instead of curse,
we respect the spark of life in everyone—
men, women, children,
animals, plants and more—
as if it were our own.

We acknowledge the life force
in our fellow travelers,
in the Earth,
in all her creatures,
and we befriend it.
As we do this,
the life essence in all things
reveals itself.
The rivers, the rain, the rocks, and the rainbows
reach out
and we discover that life is a precious thing,
a sacred thing,
a thing to be approached lovingly,

treated sweetly,
touched gently.
Countless gifts come to us
when we begin to support all life.

For the deepest desire of every one of us
is to know that we are loved,
to know that our world will feed us
and give us all that we need
just as it freely surrounds us
with the air we breathe,
the water we drink,
the land we walk upon,
constantly giving to us
like a parent to a child.

Would you turn your back upon these gifts?
Would you bring harm
unto your fellow travelers
who are more a part of you than you know?
Would you throw away the food
that nourishes your body?
Would you trample the little plants
from which your medicines are made?
Would you pour waste into your glass
before you drink of it?
Would you set fire to the trees
that bring your air

The First Intent

and shade you from the midday Sun?
Would you destroy the physical vehicle
that allows you to receive all of your gifts?

Instead, you can learn to look at life
with new eyes . . .
Come closer now
and spread the lower branches apart
so that you can peek through
and see what lies beyond.

Nature has many secrets to share with you.
Come out to where it is green,
the hills beige and brown,
the sky deepest blue.
Walk among
your woodlands and your marshes,
your parks and your beaches.
They are alive, like you.

And if in innocence you tread,
they will rejuvenate your body,
recharge your Spirit,
revitalize your world.
But you must step lightly
and discard nothing here.
Leave no destruction in your path.
Then they will open themselves to you

and welcome you
as long lost friends.

All of the things in Great Nature
and the whole of humanity
are wanting to commune with you.
But they cannot.
*Not until you change.*
Not until you see them for what they really are—
living, aware, evolving beings
just like you
who ask only that you treat them with care
so that they, in turn, can care for you.

*As a practical exercise for the First Intent, here's an idea that Lee Ching shared with me. **The next time** you're angry or frustrated about what's happening in the world, think for a few moments instead about how nice it would be if there were peace. Hold onto that thought for as long as you can, and, while you're at it, set your intent in support of all life here on this Earth. Envision peace everywhere, talk about it every chance you get, and trust that, when enough of us are intending it, we will create it and we will live in peace.*

*Harming another will never
give you the results you truly desire.*

# THE SECOND INTENT
## SEEK TRUTH

*I follow my inner compass and discard any beliefs that
are no longer serving me. I go to the source. I seek truth.*

Looking back over the course of my life, I've always
been a seeker of truth. It's been in my bones since
I was a little boy, and I never felt comfortable in a
situation where I felt deceived or confined by an illusion. As
a result, in my late twenties, I began keeping to myself back
in the hills of the Big Island in order to free myself from the
deceptions and illusions that are so prevalent in our culture.
When I did venture out into "the real world," after a period
of time in solitude, it seemed as if most of the people I ran
into weren't very happy. It was as if they'd compromised their
core values so many times that their connection with what
was best for them had all but disappeared. Instant gratifica-
tion was the name of the game, and almost everything had to

be done real quick. In short, after years of communing with Nature and then stepping back into the world, it looked like just about everyone had gone mad.

My first encounter with someone who wasn't wedded to the mainstream madness and who, like myself, sought to look deeper into the realities of life was B.J. Within a few weeks of meeting this enigmatic man at a party in Kona in 1973, he moved onto my property and started building a small coffee shack in the middle of a dense grove of tall guava trees on the upper portion of my land. One day, as we were taking a break from framing his little house, he was rolling a Bugler cigarette and talking about another aspect of the Information—seeking (and finding) the truth for ourselves. He started out by saying that most of the knowledge we'd accumulated in our lives was filled with lies. He said this included the schooling we received from day one in kindergarten, the conditioning we took on from our parents and peers, the media reports we were fed daily, and the ideas we gleaned from casual conversations with most of our fellow men and women. According to him, the powers that be who originated these lies had agendas of their own that had little to do with our happiness or well-being. He went on to explain that they were actively involved in distracting and confusing us, and that they were so proficient at what they did that it was rare for anyone to consider that other realities, beliefs, or ideas were just as valid and available to us as the ones we were being fed.

B.J.'s ideas hit home. From what he said, my mind was fair game for anyone who was more powerful than I. My problem was that I didn't have the slightest idea how to extricate myself from the ever-present clutches of the status quo. When I started to ask him about this, he said that, if I really wanted to disentangle myself from the mainstream matrix, I could begin by seeking a higher truth, a truth he said could be accessed by walking one of three paths: *the path of imitation; the path of meditation; and/or the path of experience.*

The first path, which he said was *the easiest*, required us to find someone else who was an example of all that we wanted to be and *imitate* them. He said that many of our wise elders and teachers from the past, including Jesus, Mother Mary, Buddha, Mohammed, Krishna, Lao-Tzu, White Buffalo Calf Woman, St. Germain, and all of the other Ascended Masters, had gone through the same trials and tests that we're going through and could be counted on to guide us on our quest for truth. He also recommended that I keep a copy of the *I Ching* handy. He said it was the oldest book on the planet and that, whenever I found myself in need of help, it would guide me to the highest truth. (I immediately went out and bought a copy of Carol K. Anthony's *A Guide to the I Ching* and, to this day, I carry it with me wherever I go.)

The second path, according to B.J., is the path of *meditation*. Its promise is that we can go into the stillness of our minds and, there, discover the truth about whatever we want to know. This path, which he called *the noblest*, may take some practice, but it allows us to view our surroundings and circumstances from a calmer, more detached point of view. It reveals a bigger picture to us. All we have to do in order to avail ourselves of its magic is pose a question to ourselves, quiet the activity of our minds for a few minutes, and then wait in stillness and be open to receive an answer. The better we get at stilling the clamor of our extraneous thoughts, the more quickly, he said, our answers will come to us.

The third path, which is the one taken by most people nowadays, is the path of *experience*. He called it *the bitterest*, and said that life itself will dish out the exact experiences we need to enable us to find the truth. He explained that, at first, his mentors at the Morehouse felt that this path was much too difficult for us, and they recommended that we concentrate our energies on either one of the two easier paths. But then, after carefully observing those of us who had the strength to endure the path of experience, his mentors came to the conclusion that it's how we react to our experiences that matters. They discovered that, when we approach our tests with an optimistic attitude and are completely gentle and honest with ourselves, we place ourselves in the best possible position for gaining a true understanding of our Earthly illusions. They did issue a word of caution, however: they said that it may be a little disconcerting for some of us when we discover the degree to which we've allowed ourselves to become immersed in our illusions, and that it's important for us to remember that there's nothing wrong with buying into an illusion, just as long as when we become conscious of it, we retain our freedom of choice. He said that some illusions can be fun; it's when our illusions stop working for us that we need to let them go, or learn how to stay more balanced while we're still in the midst of them.

As we sat under the guava trees smoking and swatting mosquitoes, I was totally enthralled by what he was saying. In fact, I couldn't remember anyone ever having talked to me like that before. Our conversation had risen above the every-day mundane level, and, to me, it felt as if I were being nourished. It felt like somebody cared.

He went on to say that we always have the choice of what to think, and that it is our business, and our business alone, as to what goes on between our ears. He said that there would always be people who would try to get us to buy into one illusion or another, but that, ultimately, the choice of what we believe is our own. Then, he reiterated that some illusions can be enjoyable as well as informative, and that we should take it easy on ourselves as we begin to explore them. He also repeated that it's our attitude toward them that determines how they will affect us. For instance, we could be laid off from work, not know where our next meal is coming from, and subsequently be filled with anger and despair. Or we can see the same situation from the viewpoint of someone who is glad to have a long-overdue vacation and is excited about the prospects for taking on a new line of work. He stressed that we always have the choice as to how we act (or react) toward the experiences of life. And that we're always rewarded by looking at things from a positive point of view.

I treasured B.J.'s teachings and, as I said earlier, I did my best to utilize them whenever I could. Sometimes it was easy; sometimes I failed miserably because I was too stubborn or I was missing something. Although I didn't realize it at the time,

I was still somewhat gullible and tended to give the American Dream the benefit of the doubt. It wasn't until many years later when I was writing *The Intenders of the Highest Good* that an example of a common, though particularly vicious deception came to shed more light on what B.J. had taught me. I received it in the form of a curious download one afternoon while I was sitting quietly on my front porch in Hawaiian Beaches. I'm not sure where it came from; all I know is that, for a period of about ten minutes, the illusions of security and insurance were laid bare before me. At first, this knowledge was so startling that I left it out of the final edit of my first novel. I share it with you now because, after long reflection, I've become convinced that buying into some illusions can be downright harmful.

Here are my notes from that morning.

*We've been taught, from the time we were small children, that bad things can happen to us, but that if we have insurance we will be protected against them. The people who sell us this question-able product are made out to be knights in shining armor, assuring us that they will always be there for us if, God forbid, we have a fender bender, or something is stolen from us, or a hurricane hits our home, or one of our loved ones dies. Never mind that the knight's armor is a little tarnished because his first motivation is not to help us out, but to put more food on his own table; likewise, never mind that the insurance companies, next to the banks, are the richest corporations in the world; and never mind that they have jumped into bed with their political and media cronies and made it illegal for us to go without some of their dubious products and services; and, above all, never mind that, in order to get us to* buy into their illusions and deceptions, the insurance companies plant the seeds of fear into our hearts and minds and do their level best to keep that fear growing and thriving as much as possible.

The thinking processes we go through when we buy into the illusion/deception of insurance are very interesting, albeit insensible. In order to even entertain the idea of purchasing an insurance policy, and not discard it immediately, we have to be holding firmly onto an image in our minds of ourselves involved in some sort of tragedy. Why we would want to do this, in light of the powerful effects our thoughts have on our lives, is a mystery of the human condition. Suffice it to say, we have to be envisioning ourselves in a car wreck or suffering a loss if we're going to consider buying an insurance policy. Just as when we invite an attack to ourselves because we take a defensive position, we also invite accidents and losses into our lives when we buy insurance. Our thoughts do turn into our 3-D experiences, and it is for us to discern and look deeper into the mechanics of how these thoughts are affecting us.

Do we really want to pay out a large portion of our hard-earned money to someone just so we can continue to perpetuate our own tragedies? It sounds crazy, but that's exactly what we do when we sign up for an insurance policy. We allow another to play upon our fears—most often, our worst fears—not realizing that, by envisioning our accidents, we are in the process of creating them.

The truth of the matter is that we'd all be much better off without any insurance. We'd have a lot more ready cash in our pockets; we'd live in a lot less fear; we'd create far less suffering for ourselves; and we'd open the door for true peace of mind to step in and bless our lives. Anyone who questions this should take a moment and *look at it from a slightly different perspective. Wouldn't we drive a lot more safely if there weren't any automobile insurance? If we knew we had to pay for our car repairs, not to mention our medical bills, out of our own pockets, wouldn't we slow down and be more responsible drivers? When you really think about it, doesn't our reliance upon the insurance companies make it easier for us to pay less attention to our driving and, as such, suffer more accidents on our streets and highways?*

*Our challenge is that, for many of us, letting go of our dependence on insurance, even after we've thoroughly realized that it isn't serving us anymore, isn't as easy as it sounds. It calls for us to set our victim-like behavior aside and take greater responsibility for our actions. It asks us to turn our thinking processes around by putting our attention on that which we truly want for ourselves and ignore the persistent sales efforts of those who would deceive us for their own personal gain. Ultimately, in order to rid ourselves of this insidious deception, we will have to summon our courage and have faith that, when we hold the thought that we are loved and protected by the Universe in each and every moment of our lives, that is what we will create. Said another way, from the minute we're able to hold our thoughts on that which we truly desire, we will no longer have need of a system of insurance that begs us to depend upon others to provide us with a kind of false security. Instead of fantasizing about disasters, we will begin to experience and enjoy the true security that comes from a knowing within.*

From the moment I received this information, I was no longer as suggestible as before. I began to look even deeper into any new ideas that came to me, not with an attitude of skepticism, but with an attitude of discernment. *I simply intended to know whether something served me or not.*

Here is another example of a common deception that haunts our world today:

*It always seems strange to me to go to a sporting event in a large stadium or auditorium and, when they play the national anthem, almost everyone in the crowd stands up and holds their hand over their hearts, on the left side of their chest. The same thing happens when you go into a classroom today and see the children saying the pledge of allegiance to the flag while holding their hands over a spot on the left side of their chests, thinking that that is where their hearts are.*

*But WAIT A MINUTE! That's not where our hearts are at all. Our hearts are in the exact center of our chests, both anatomically and spiritually. No matter what the doctors, teachers, sports enthusiasts, or children tell you, your heart is in the middle, just as if your body were aligned on a cross. The exact center-point where the horizontal and vertical axes meet is where your heart lies.*

*I've even spoken with young children about this and they will swear that their hearts are on the left side, and when I asked them how they knew that to be true, they said that their teacher told them so.*

*So what is the purpose in deceiving so many people from a very young age about the correct placement of their hearts? It is because our hearts are a very special focal point. It is where we connect to all the Love in the Universe. However, if we can't find it, or think it* is somewhere where it isn't, then it becomes harder for us to come into contact with the true Love of God. And it is much easier for us to be controlled.

It sounds crazy, but, on a very subtle level, when we lose track of the location of our hearts, it becomes more difficult for us to send and receive Love. For thousands of years, there has been a deliberate, concerted effort to hide our hearts from us so that we could be manipulated more easily. But now we are beginning to see through all of the deceptions that are constantly being perpetrated upon humanity, and we are finding our hearts and all the Love that resides there. For it is in the center of our hearts where all of the things we search for, all of the treasures we travel far and wide to find, all the successes we toil for lifetimes to achieve, all the most sacred sites and the sweetest feelings are to be found. For those who are still skeptical, I suggest that you hold your undivided attention on the exact center of your chest for a while and see what happens.

Gradually, as I received more information like this, my intuition started to awaken. And then, almost miraculously, I was given another tool that enabled me to go to the source of the issues and illusions that were presenting themselves to me. It arose out of a conversation I had in Sebastopol, California, with my Cherokee friend, Neal.

Neal is a powerful seer who lives on the central coast of California. One cloudy autumn afternoon, he and I were sitting on the front porch of a mutual friend's home, talking—if that's what you want to call it. You see, Neal is a man of few words. Very few words. It's just that, when he does say something, I feel as if I'm in the presence of great wisdom.

On this particular day, he and I had been sitting quietly for about twenty minutes after I'd asked him what he thought we most needed to do to further ourselves along our spiritual paths. Finally, following a lengthy deliberation, he looked over at me and said one word:

"**Purification**."

To which I immediately responded by asking what he meant by that.

Another five minutes or so went by without a word. Then he stood up, stretched like a cat, and said that purification could be achieved by doing three things. The first requires us to learn how to discern what is good for us and what isn't. To do this, he said, we need to find our Yes and our No inside ourselves. Again, I asked him what he meant, and he said that it was something he couldn't really define; he could only tell me how it worked in his own life. He went on to elaborate, saying that, when he wanted to know whether something was good for him or not, he would make a statement to himself (as opposed to asking himself a question). The beginning of the statement, he said, was always the same: "**It's in my highest and best good if I** ... go to town, eat such and such a food, take a particular pill, meet with so and so, buy a certain item, and so forth." In fact, he said that, nowadays, no matter what he was going to do, he always made this statement and then waited for a response to come.

At first, he said he couldn't always trust the responses that came back. But with patience (which was his strong suit) and steady practice, he started to get the hang of it. Also, he said that, after a while, the way the responses came to him started to change. In the beginning, after he stated that it was in his Highest Good for him to watch a particular movie, for example, when the response was a Yes, the index finger of his left hand would twitch a little bit. He demonstrated this by sitting straight up with his hands placed flat on his knees and moving his left hand index finger in a quick, jerking motion. Likewise, if the guidance was a No, which indicated for him to go no further with whatever he was inquiring about, the index finger on his right hand would twitch.

He said that the responses went on this way for several months, and then they suddenly changed. Instead of his fingers twitching, his head started to move. If the response was a Yes, his head would raise slightly, like he was looking up at something in the sky. And if it was a No, his head nodded forward, like he was looking down at the ground just in front of his feet.

Everything stayed this way for a long time and then, one day, it shifted again into the method he's still using today. Now it isn't a part of his body that moves when he seeks discernment. Instead, he begins to get a specific feeling and he hears a voice inside his head that expresses how he feels. Eventually, he learned to put all of his trust in this voice, and it works like this: He makes the statement about the Highest Good as usual, and if the response is a Yes, he hears the word "Aaaahhh!" clearly inside his head. And if it's a No, he hears the single syllable, "Yuck!"

I couldn't help but laugh, and he even chuckled a little himself. But before he was quiet again, he said that each of us has our Yes and our No—our "Aaaahhh!" and our "Yuck!"—inside of us, and

*that our lives would go much more smoothly if we would start to*
*get to know them better.*

After my conversation with Neal, I began practicing discernment in earnest by putting my intuition, muscle testing,
dowsing rods, and a pendulum to work. My favorite was a
pendulum that an Intender in Seattle had given to me when
I was on tour several years earlier. To this day, it continues to
help me, because I can use it to answer just about every question I have. By checking with it to see if something is for my
highest and best good, not only am I able to purify myself, but
I am also better able to spot the illusions and deceptions that
permeate our world today.

A seeker of truth
must ask questions:
What if? Am I? Am I not?
These are the tools we use
as we wade through worlds
of illusion and deception
seeking answers where others are complacent,
resolution where others are confused,
peace where others are conflicted.

We dig deeper,
search further,
not content
until what we have found
feels right.

Seek Truth

Three kinds of illusions exist:
the major and minor illusions
and the predatory deceptions.

Of the major illusions there are five:
Solid, Separate, Self, Gender, and Time.
These represent who or what we think we are
but not who we really are.
To find out who we really are
we must begin to identify
with something new,
something finer,
something magnificent,
something spiritual.

For in truth
we are Spirit,
not solid but formless,
not separate but connected,
not fixed but flexible,
not our physical selves but more . . .
an Essence wisping in the wind,
a Ghost shifting its shape,
a Being living forever.

If you doubt,
ask these questions:
Am I solid

or am I made up of atoms and molecules
with vast spaces between?
Am I separate
or am I One with All That Is,
afloat in an endless etheric substance?
Am I my name
or can I be any name I choose?
Am I my body
or the wondrous Being
that lives inside it,
free to dwell in all places,
to explore other worlds,
to fly with the eagles?
Am I man or woman
or am I both
on the inside?
Am I not everything I want to be
on the inside?

Time is another make-believe game
that is best kept in perspective.
It can help with business
and social obligations,
to gather and meet with friends,
but other than that
its uses are so limited
as to hinder our way.

Seek Truth

Does time really exist
in the world of matter
or is it something
that comes from our minds
and from our agreements with others?
Does the wolf or the mountain lion
have need of a calendar?
Does the woods-person need a clock
other than the Sun or Moon?
Are not the past and future
places within us
not to be seen
through our Earthly eyes?

Is it worth it to be so caught up
in our schedules and appointments
that we miss hearing the call of the wild bird,
seeing the lightning flash on the distant horizon,
tasting the sweet nectars of life,
feeling the warmth of the Sun on our faces,
or the subtle blessing offered by the river
when we stand with our feet
in her cool water?

The minor illusions are even more worldly,
more social and subject to change.
They are Age, Family, Occupation,
Possession, Race, Religion, and Nationality.

The Second Intent

And not one of them is real
*unless we make it so.*

*Age*
In our search for truth we must ask:
What is our true age?
Can the Being inside of us get older?
Or is it only the body that ages?
Are there not drawbacks
to identifying with our age?
Does not the body of those
who hold onto this illusion
take on the characteristics
of that age?
We add to our wrinkles and gray
lest we become more aware
of our thoughts and our words.

Is it not better
to be ageless?
Isn't that what we really are anyway—
an Essence in Eternity
ever full of youth?

*Family*
Who is our real family, our true tribe?
Are they kin from the same blood?
Are they clan who share similar interests?
Or are they larger still,

going back to days of old,
coming from other worlds?
Who are our true brothers and sisters,
our Mother and our Father?
How many tribes do we belong to?

As we seek truth
our family expands.
It starts small, within the bloodline,
then one day we realize
that a friend is like family to us
or perhaps closer.
We share at a deeper level with this person
and a bigger picture emerges.
Intuitively, we remember
that we were meant to be together,
that we planned it
and that we are a part of a much larger tribe,
a group of souls
who travel across time and space
united by common ideas and projects
and goals.

The more we identify
with ourselves as Spirit
and the more we commune
with Great Oneness,
the more we will discover

The Second Intent

about our tribes
until we reach a day
when no matter where we go
they are always with us,
and we realize that
there is no one outside of our tribe.

*Occupation*
Our careers may be our life's work
but they are not to be confused
with who we are.
Occupations limit our horizons
but our skills are limitless,
expanding
with every new lesson we learn,
with every new person we meet,
with every new step we walk upon this Earth.
If, like the babe who clings to the nest,
we stay in one occupation too long,
we outgrow our surroundings
and begin to feel discomfort.
Our wise ancestors always taught
that we should do our work
only until we get good at it.
Then, go on to the next thing.
In this way, we gain many skills.
Let not our identification with our careers
imprison us

Seek Truth

and keep us from amassing
a wide variety of skills.

Remember . . . you are not your job.
You are all jobs
waiting to be mastered.

*Possession*
The things that surround us
that we call our own,
to what extent are they really ours?

What do we do when they are lost,
or break,
or are taken away?
How strong is the thread
that runs from our inner peace
to the thing that we think we own?
And if it is gone,
do we get upset?

When our security is tied to our possessions,
we limit ourselves
in ways we do not see.
We hold on tightly to our stuff
and cart it around
or store it away at great cost,
thinking it cannot be replaced.
We empower our weaknesses

The Second Intent

and keep our faith at bay.
But those who trust
that all things can be manifested
and will be there when they are needed
are secure.
They do not require pieces of paper,
or handshakes,
or indebtedness of any kind
to feel better about themselves.

Our true security comes
not from the mountains of material goods
we have accumulated,
but from the knowing
that if we let something go
it can still come back to us.

*Race*
Our wise ancestors taught their young children
the difference between appearances and content.
That we cannot tell what is inside of something
or someone
by outward appearances.
How many products have we purchased
because of what was on the box,
only to discover
that what was on the inside
was not what we thought it was going to be?

Seek Truth

It is the same with people.
We cannot know what is going on
inside of them
by the way they look.
But there are some things
that we can know about them.
Each one is Spirit.
Each one wants a good life.
And each one is equal
in the eyes of Great Oneness
regardless of skin color,
or race,
or bone structure.

These are characteristics of the body,
not of the Being inside.
Not of the Beings we truly are.

*Religion*
The Spirit inside of us grows and expands
as we embrace all things.
We can say that we are Christians or Jews,
Catholics, Muslims, Hindus, or Baha'is.
But that is not who we are.
It is only what we identify with.
In truth, we are Spirit unlimited,
encased in a body,
infused with countless beliefs,

wandering
and returning homeward
again and again.

It is good to gather with others
in the Name of God
to ignite the spark of Oneness within us.
And it is wise to connect with a Teacher
who will fan the flames of Love in our hearts.

But these acts
do not define us.
They deliver us.

*Nationality*
Our country asks that we make agreements
with those we know
and those we don't know
about arbitrary boundaries
and what goes on inside of them.
We mark territories
that are unbounded,
stake claims
that are unfounded,
and rally around a set of principles
in the name of something
that does not exist
except on paper
and in the minds of those who profit from it.

Seek Truth

We must ask ourselves:
Does the Sun shine brighter
on one side of a boundary line than the other?
Do the rains fall harder
on us than on our neighbors?
Does the coyote or the hawk pay heed
to our borders?
Do the storm clouds let up
because they approach our shores?

The time will come
when we will no longer need our boundaries,
when we will see that they keep us apart
instead of together.
We will come to the point
when we will respect everyone else
no matter where they live.
And we will see through
the sham of patriotism
for what it truly is—
a means for those who are more aggressive
to control us,
to keep us living in fear,
and to get us to fight their fights.

But, one day soon
the fighting will stop
and we will come together

The Second Intent

and our borderlines will be erased
because we will not need them
in a world
where people love and care for each other.

*The Predatory Deceptions*
The Ancestors of old also spoke
of a large group of thought patterns
they called the predatory deceptions.
They said that within
the collective thoughts of the world
were numerous ideas and beliefs
that made people feel insecure
and rendered them easy prey
for those who would take their energy away.

To walk the path of truth,
one must come face to face
with these deceptions
and see them for what they are—
an effort to keep us off balance
and feeling less than
who we really are.
It is as if we are being held tightly
in the claws of a strong predator
that will not let go of us.

To be free
we must begin to distance ourselves

Seek Truth

from our basic beliefs about
poverty, defense, security,
self-worth, guilt, loneliness,
and more.

It is important to remember
that the predatory deceptions
cannot hold onto to us
when we know
our thoughts create our world
and we can think anything we like.
That is our choice.
That is our point of reference.
That is our true security.
And that is what
awakens our Spirits.

To disentangle ourselves
once and forever
from the predator's claws,
we must reject all suggestions
that we are anything but abundant
lest we draw poverty to us,

that we need to put up a defense
lest we draw an attack to us,

that we need to purchase insurance
lest we draw calamity to us,

that we are undeserving
lest we draw scarcity to us,

that we are guilty
lest we draw worry to us,

that we are alone
lest we draw helplessness to us.

Like the shadow that passes
in front of the Moon
and darkens our way,
the illusions and deceptions that hover
between us and our Spirits
hide that which we truly are.
But this will not last.

For, just as the winds rise before dawn
and push the clouds
out from between us and the celestial bodies,
so will the truth rise
and push away the illusions of life,
allowing our Spirits to shine forth,
revealing to all
that we are innocent children of God,
equal in His eyes,
with everyone and everything else
having access to all good things,
surrounded always by friends in many realms,

Seek Truth

free to experience,
explore,
and enjoy
All That Is.

*Each and everyone of us is powerful beyond measure. That is the truth. Yet one of the greatest barriers that stands between ourselves and our power arises out of our habit of thinking that others are better than we are. We harbor the illusion of a low self-image. With this in mind,* **the next time** *you find yourself putting someone else on a pedestal and wishing you were like them, give yourself equal time. See yourself up on that same pedestal, happy and deserving of all good things. Hold that thought until you're comfortable with it. Hold it until you feel it in your heart of hearts—and watch your life begin to change.*

*The more vigilant you become in observing your thoughts without attaching any emotion to them, and the better you get at turning the ones that aren't working for you around, the more you will liberate yourself from the prison of your own self-imposed limitations. People will automatically be more attracted to you. And when they ask what's helped you make such a positive difference in your life, you can tell them it was the truth that set you free.*

*Our challenges are there
in order to lead us to a greater awareness.*

# THE THIRD INTENT
## SET YOUR COURSE

*I begin the creative process. I give direction to my life.*
*I set my course.*

After watching thousands of people make and manifest their intentions over the years, we began to notice a common thread. We saw that those who started out their day by setting their intentions had an entirely different experience than those who didn't. Their life had a direction to it. Things came more easily to them. They struggled less and had more moments of pure joy because that's how you feel when your desires are being fulfilled.

*The circumstances that brought the four original Intenders together is a magical story in itself. It all started one rainy day just outside of Keaau, Hawaii, with my girlfriend Betsy and me standing on the side of the road under a small umbrella, hitchhiking. Neither one of* us had a car at the time; mine was in the shop and Betsy didn't need one. Before going any further, let me say that, up to that point in my life, Betsy Palmer Whitney was the most extraordinary woman I'd ever met. If Tina was the spiritual guide for our small circle, it was Betsy who was the power. Blind since the age of two, she could manifest anything. In fact, you never told Betsy that there was something she couldn't do because, invariably, she'd turn right around and do it. When she intended to have an office full of specialized, state-of-the-art computer equipment, it came so fast it made my head spin. When we needed a publisher, Betsy created Dolphin Press (which has since become one of the country's foremost Braille transcribers). Whenever I'd get stuck on a project and start complaining, "How do I get this #@%*&! thing to work?" it was always Betsy who'd answer, "Hey Tony, why don't you just intend it?"

And that's what she did when we were standing out there on the side of the road in Keaau. It was raining like crazy, both of us were getting soaked because my umbrella wasn't big enough, and not a car had come by for at least fifteen minutes. I started to grumble and Betsy calmly said, "Why don't we intend that we have a ride now?" I said okay, we made our intention, and less than a minute later, a blue Toyota pickup pulled up, loaded with boxes, books, and more odd-looking stuff than you can imagine. Inside the cab were my old friends, Mark and Tina. They'd just finished working the flea market in Hilo and were on the way to their new home in Paradise Park.

With the four of us crowded like sardines in the front seat—I distinctly remember my face wedged up against the window glass for part of the trip—I introduced Betsy and told her that I'd known Mark and Tina from when they lived across the street from my mother in Kailua, Kona, three years earlier. We'd become good friends then and had even worked several dozen craft fairs around the island together, but had lost track of each other after moving to the other side of the island.

Well, the three of them hit it off right away (even though Betsy was practically sitting on top of Tina), and they ended up driving us several miles out of their way to our place in Hawaiian Beaches. When we got there, we invited them in and, over the next couple of hours, we caught up on old times, laughed a lot, and shared a meal together. When it came time for them to go, Betsy asked if they'd like to come back again soon, and they agreed.

Tina called during the middle of the week and, on the following Sunday evening, they returned with a big bowl of salad and a bunch of other scrumptious goodies that Mark had whipped together. We ate like royalty and, after dinner, I happened to mention the intention that Betsy made right before they picked us up in the rain the week before. This brought up the subjects of manifestation and empowerment, and I truly don't recall how it came about, but, within a short time, the four of us were sitting in a circle on Betsy's back porch saying our intentions.

That was the first Intenders Circle, and I do remember that we felt so squeamish about what we were doing at first that we even joked about it. But, of course, later on, after our intentions began to manifest, we didn't joke about it anymore. We just said how grateful we were to be a part of something so special.

The next couple of years were pure fun. Our little circle grew, and it was common to have the room filled with people on

Sunday evenings. Something we began to notice right away was that our Intenders Circles usually had a number of artists and entrepreneurs in them, and it wasn't long before we found out why. In one of our spiritual guidance sessions, Mother Mary, who, by that time, had started coming through Betsy, told us that artists, entrepreneurs, and Intenders were a creative lot who were interested in making something out of nothing. They enjoyed taking ideas that were inside their minds and bringing them to life. She told us that every man and woman on Earth is creating their reality every day, but that there is a big difference between what the average person is doing and what The Intenders are doing. She said that most people are not creating consciously or deliberately, like we were. She emphasized that the truly creative person who has an idea and makes an intention around it is taking their destiny into their own hands, while those who have not yet learned to *intend* go through life at the mercy of forces outside themselves.

With the help of Mother Mary, Lee Ching, and many others who magically showed up in our spiritual guidance sessions during those years, we developed and refined the Intention Process. The Intention Process began with us making a simple, clear intention and ended up with our desires manifesting before us. Each morning, we'd set the course for our day by saying something like: "I intend that I am _____," (and we'd fill in the blank with whatever we desired). For example, we might say, "I intend that I am happy and healthy," and/or "I intend that I am in a wonderful relationship with someone who loves me as much as I love them," and/or "I intend that I have a new refrigerator." Then we'd invoke the Highest Good, say "So be it and so it is," and follow that up by *being open to receive and grateful in advance* for what was coming to us.

Those of us who have been with The Intenders since the beginning have seen countless people manifest their intentions. Week after week, our friends who previously felt disempowered blossomed right in front of our eyes as they told their success stories. Their doubts were vanishing because now they had a reliable system that was making their lives better.

As we learned more about making our intentions, we realized that setting a course in the morning gives a positive direction to one's day. We also found that, if we stated our intentions in a circle of friends once a week, our week went along much better than if we missed the circle. When we got together and talked about what we were witnessing, we all agreed that we were truly blessed to have received this empowering information. There was only one problem: *remembering to use it.*

## — *An Intenders Story* —

*If you forget to say your intentions in the morning, you can still say them later. In fact, you can set your intent anytime you need to create or manifest something. I recall a time last year when a friend of mine and I were pulling into a large parking lot early one Saturday evening to rent a video. Every space, for as far as we could see, was filled. Normally, we would have made an intention on the way to the video store by saying something like, "I intend we have a great place to park when we get there." Then we'd invoke the Highest Good and say "So be it and so it is."*

*But we forgot to do that, and as we looked around and I almost started to voice a complaint, my friend suddenly remembered, then quickly stated an intention, said "So be it"—and just as she did, a brown conversion van backed out of the space directly in front of the main door to the store. I got so excited that I yelled out, "And there it is!"*

*She pulled into the spot and both of us sat there laughing. Our "So be it and so it is" had turned into "So be it and there it is." We'd had a conscious instantaneous manifestation, and it was as if we'd received a confirmation that we were evolving to our next step. I can't tell you how good it felt.*

*Mark Shapiro*
*Los Angeles, CA*

When we set an intention
we enter the world of the magical.
By stating our word boldly
we draw unseen forces
to work on our behalf.
Many do not believe this.
They discount the miraculous
and say that it does not work.
But they are missing out.

The Third Intent

Our thoughts and words
are powerful.
They are active
and very energetic.
Used unconsciously
or with disrespect
they bring chaos.

Intent is a very special ally.
It is a friend to man and woman,
a harbinger who readies,
a helper who gathers,
an artist who shapes and forms
the quantum substances
so that they may
materialize
and manifest
miraculously
before us.

How do you approach
this powerful companion
so that you know
you will work wisely together?
You single out a desire,
any desire.

Make sure it is one
that you really want to experience.

Set Your Course

Then call forth the Highest Good
(so that only the intentions
that serve you will manifest)
and then clearly,
courageously,
confidently
speak aloud
the dreams of your heart.
Intend that they come to you,
then let them go and know that
Great Oneness is taking care of everything
from then on.

After that, all that is required
is to remain alert,
be ready to receive
and know:
when you set your intent
for that which you seek to create,
it will be created.

The exercises for the Third Intent are all hands-on, practical exercises designed to provide results right away. In fact, Lee Ching told us one evening that our Intenders Circles always had angelic beings and guides who gathered around them, and that these helpers saw to it that the newcomers' first few intentions were manifested quickly and in such a way that they couldn't be missed. He called it a *Beginner's Luck Factor*;

but, as we were learning, it wasn't really luck. It was a law that calls forth special helpers from the invisible realms to serve anyone who sets an intention for the Highest Good.

*And so . . . **the next time** you get up in the morning, before you leave the house, stop and set your course for the day by making several intentions. Get them as clear as you can—and make them only once a day (unless you happen to be in a circle of friends later on who are also setting their intentions, then you can say them again).*

1. *Make at least one or two intentions for a physical object. Have it be something you need and remember to intend that you're open to receive it from both expected and unexpected sources.*
2. *Set a clear intention for your environment. For instance, you might intend that our air, water, and soil are completely pure. Or that mankind is living in peace. Get as creative as you like.*
3. *Make at least one or two intentions for an emotional experience. Perhaps it will be for a relationship, or for a state of joy to embrace you. On this one, be sure to find the positive way to say it. Don't say, "I intend that I am not angry anymore." Instead, say, "I intend that I am tolerant and emotionally balanced at all times."*
4. *Make an intention or two about your expanding mental faculties. It could be that you desire to enhance your memory, or that you connect with a higher source of wisdom. Anything that expands your thinking outside of its customary processes*

will do. A good example of this is, "Knowing that my thoughts are the forerunners of my experiences, I intend that I am more vigilant of my thoughts, and that I am keeping my attention only on thoughts that serve me and my world."

5. Make an intention or two regarding your spiritual growth. Perhaps you'd like to intend that your next step is clearly revealed to you. Or that you experience yourself as a spiritual being becoming fully conscious. Or that you feel the true love of God in your life. Intend whatever seems appropriate for you at this time, but make certain that it is something that you really want—because you're going to get it!

(Note: This chapter only contains a few of the basic fundamentals of intentionality. If you'd like to expand your knowledge on the subject, we refer you to *The Intenders Handbook: A Guide to the Intention Process and the Conscious Community*. This little booklet is full of information about how to set your course.)

*Everything in your world—*
*the world at large*
*as well as your individual world,*
*including everything you see,*
*hear, smell, taste, touch, and feel—*
*is the result of a thought manifestation.*

# THE FOURTH INTENT
## SIMPLIFY

*I let go so there is room for something better to come in.
I intend that I am guided, guarded, protected, and lined
up with the Highest Good at all times. I trust and remain
open to receive from both expected and unexpected
sources. I simplify.*

As The Intenders began to grow, we talked a lot about trust. We all agreed that there is no issue more important in these transitional times than trust, and that each of us, in our own mysterious way, is faced with the decision whether or not to trust that our thoughts will, in fact, manifest as we intend them. We also had to decide whether to believe that a higher power was working behind the scenes of our lives. And each was confronted with choosing, at one time or another, whether to let go of whatever we were attached to, lest we remain stagnant and stuck in the mud of our old ways.

There is a short story Lee Ching told us that helped to bring the principle of simplifying our lives into focus. He said that, if we're going to cross over a small stream and see what adventures await us on the other side, eventually we have to leave the side we're standing on and step across the water. According to him, most people are living as if they have a foot on each side of the stream, straddling it, while the water level is rising. If they don't make a move pretty soon, they're going to get wet.

This little analogy works on many levels. It relates to cleaning our homes insofar as, if we don't let go of some of the old stuff that's been lying around for years, we may never have room for any new stuff to come in. Likewise, it can also pertain to ideas we're carrying around with us. As we move closer to the cultural transition that looms on the horizon, we're beginning to discover that many of our beliefs and ideas aren't serving us anymore. They're outdated or barely working, and we really can't count on them like we used to. Most of the information we're being fed by the media fits into this category. An example, although it may not always be stated outright, is that being at war will make things better. This archaic idea no longer works for us, and it really never did. All caring, thinking people know that we simply cannot achieve peace as long as we support war, and yet war is still the cornerstone upon which the foundation of our entire civilization is built. If, however, we truly want peace—*if we intend that we have true and lasting peace*—we must let go of our tendency to make war and replace it with a more positive approach of resolving our differences. We must let it go so that something new and better can come in.

The same is true of our beliefs surrounding money. We've been taught that the larger our bank account is, the more secure we'll be, and that everything we need will be there for us just as long as we have enough money. Unfortunately, an inherent weakness lies hidden within this kind of thinking. On a very subtle level, our money supply is being systematically tampered with, causing those who have unknowingly put their eggs in the money basket to be squeezed like never before. Many people who once counted on their money to take care of them are now finding out what it's like to be without it. This scenario does have a positive side, however. As unsettling as it is, running out of cash may be just what we need to stop us from relying so heavily on money so that we can begin to look elsewhere for our security.

For security, in the truest sense, is the peace of mind and quietude of heart that comes from inside of us. *It is not inherently dependent on our financial status, but is a strength we gain by knowing that whatever we need will be there for us in the exact moment we need it.* In these changing times, each and every one of us, on one level or another, is in the process of integrating this bit of wisdom into our consciousness and, along the way, we're learning to trust at a much deeper level than we've ever trusted before. Soon, we'll manifest whatever we want instantaneously, but, as of yet, we cannot step over the stream and take advantage of our potential abilities until we let go (or at least *are willing* to let go) of money as the means by which we measure our security.

At our early Intenders Circles, the subject of money came up a lot, and several of us were deeply concerned about the fact that so many of our fellow travelers had allowed their happiness to become dependent upon what's in their pocketbooks. Intuitively, we knew that the Universe wants us to be happy and secure, but that its hands are tied as long·as we continue to hold on so tightly to our money. The only way we could see to resolve this dilemma was by becoming so empowered that we could manifest anything at will. In the meantime, while we were waiting, we could learn how to be happy whether we had money or not. This was easier for some of us than others because only a handful of us *knew* that our intentions could just as easily come from unexpected sources that didn't necessarily involve the use of money. Of course, this route took great trust, as well as patience, on our part, but we could see that, in the long run, we would all breathe a sigh of relief and have a good laugh because, eventually, we'd become so proficient at manifesting that it wouldn't matter anymore how much money we had in our pockets.

*There's a story I'd tell my friends in San Diego after I settled there about the twenty-five years I lived out in the country on the Big Island of Hawaii. They always had a hard time believing it; nevertheless, it happened to me, and it's all true.*

*When I purchased my property on the slopes of Mauna Loa in upcountry Kona in 1973, the nearest town was several miles away and, except for one old funky country store, goods and services were not readily available. I was spending my days working on the farm with B.J. and one of the things he told me was that everything I needed (and most of the things I wanted) would come to me. He* said that I didn't need to go anywhere if I didn't want to. All I had to do was believe it. I could stay at home as much as I liked, but there was one hitch: I'd have to learn to be patient.

I remember him saying, "You don't have to know how or from whom the things you need will come. In fact, expecting that things will arrive from a specific source tends to work against you because that's what closes the door for things to come to you from unexpected sources. All you have to know is that they will come to you when you need them."

At first, I scoffed at the idea. I'd always been taught that I had to work hard, earn a lot of money, apply a lot of effort, then I would get what I wanted. I didn't know anything about intentionality back then and, because everything was going so well for me at the time, I had no inclination to test anything new. It turned out, however, that during my second year there, I lost my job and my car broke down at the same time. I was resigned to hitchhiking or staying at home in my small coffee shack for months on end. Most people would have started to panic, but, since I was single and a little reclusive anyway, it gave me the opportunity to put B.J.'s idea to the test.

So I got up one morning and told myself that everything I needed would be there for me when I needed it. I didn't have to worry or stress. On the contrary, I'd be nonchalant and trust that, in some way unknown to me, I was being helped. I decided, then and there, to really believe it without waffling or wavering, and otherwise enjoy my day doing the things I liked to do.

It started working right away! My makeshift coffee shack was 600 feet up a steep, rocky, densely forested hill, but that didn't keep anybody away. When I needed car parts, a friend surprised me

*one day with a trunk-load of them. When I needed food, it was left
mysteriously at the bottom of the trail to my place. When I needed
company, all sorts of people came to visit. I even remember one full-
moon evening when a pretty lady showed up unexpectedly with a
large pizza and a bottle of wine.*

*As more and more of these things happened, my belief got
stronger. And so did my patience. Over the years, I realized that my
needs were always met. I gained confidence in the knowledge that I
was always provided for. And I also saw that, when I was stressing
out about something, my problems were most often in my mind and
not in my immediate environment. Sometimes I think back to the
time when B.J. told me about all this and how crazy I thought he
was. But, as it turned out, he wasn't crazy at all. He was wise.*

To me, Mark Dziatko embodies the attitude of trust as much
as anyone I've ever met. Mark (he's the handsome one on The
Intenders video) was the youngest and most self-assured of
the four original Intenders. Whenever any of us needed anything, we'd always ask Mark about it first, because we knew
he'd either have it, or he'd come up with it right away.

As Mark described it, he was in the "recycling" business,
which meant that he would go to garage sales, take away other
people's junk, fix it, clean it up, and sell it to someone who
really needed it. This creative line of work always provided
him with a comfortable living near the beach and, in fact, he'd
even built his house out of recycled materials.

One thing I noticed about Mark as we worked together
over the years was that he was always alert, resourceful, ready

to receive, and confident that his intentions were manifesting. Not once did he ever show doubt or expect that they wouldn't. Later on, when eBay came along, he became a pioneer in the online auction business, and when I'd ask him how he was doing, he'd always make a point of telling me how simple it was to go to the post office to mail things and pick up checks from people around the country.

I remember one day when Mark and I and our friend Aaron were putting a roof on his house in the Waa Waa subdivision, down the red road that parallels the eastern coast of the Big Island. He was talking about our empowerment and what it would take for us to realize our highest potential. He said that everyone has the same God-given abilities to create, and that, since we can all think, we can all put our thoughts to work on our behalf. Those who are conscious of this information may appear to have a head start at manifesting, but everyone can do it because we all enjoy the same access to our power.

Then he shifted gears and started talking about the Highest Good, saying that we could make all the intentions in the world, but if we didn't line up with the Highest Good, we were looking for trouble. He said that that was the biggest problem with the world today: many people were accessing their power, but they weren't using it for the Highest Good. Having power without a strong connection with the Highest Good was a dangerous thing, he said.

I was hanging on his every word. These ideas resonated deep within me and, in fact, they were the building blocks of what was later to become the Intention Process. They also explained why some of the things I'd manifested recently didn't seem to be working out so well. I hadn't incorporated the Highest Good into my intentions. Mark said that this was a common oversight, and he pointed out that there are all sorts of things we think we want, but that sometimes it's difficult for us to tell in advance which ones are good for us and which ones aren't. He said that we can avoid getting ourselves involved in uncomfortable situations by including the Highest Good clause at the end of our intentions.

He further explained that by saying something like *"in order for my intentions to manifest, they must serve the Highest Good of the Universe, myself, and everyone everywhere,"* (and knowing that what I say is what I'll get), I can be assured that only the intentions that are aligned with my Highest Good will come into manifestation. Any that are born out of shadowy, selfish, or unserving motives will remain unmanifested.

*We had an example of this a while back in our Intenders Circle with a lady named Genie who kept making the same intention week after week. She intended that she is in a relationship with the man of her dreams, and, week after week, we expected her to arrive at the circle with her new boyfriend on her arm. But, after several months, it still hadn't happened.*

*So, one evening after we'd finished our intentions and gratitudes, Mark asked Lee Ching why Genie's intention hadn't manifested yet. The answer he received was quite profound. He was told that it simply wasn't in Genie's (or her future boyfriend's) highest and best interests to have a man come into her life at this time; that she didn't really have the handle on her negativity yet; and that if he were to show up in her life, she wouldn't be able, at her present level of emotional maturity, to keep him around. It was suggested that she do some more work on herself to keep calmer and more centered in the midst of life's little storms, and, in this way, when the man of her dreams did come along, she'd be better prepared to make the most of the relationship.*

Another thing I always admired about Mark was his relaxed attitude toward life—how he worked hard, but never seemed to be in a hurry. When I asked him how he stayed so calm, he said that he didn't allow himself to get too attached to specific outcomes, especially where time was concerned. He said that letting go and patience go hand in hand, and that we need to understand that our timing and the Universe's timing are two different things. Our manifestations, he said, really can come at the last minute. But, if we interfere with the Intention Process by doubting, cutting corners, or stressing and striving, we lose the chance of seeing what would have happened if we'd waited a little longer. In fact, he said, as hard as it is to get used to, there are times when it's definitely in our Highest Good to have things come to us at the last minute. How else, he asked, would we learn about trust? How else would we gain the inner strength necessary to take the next step in our evolution? He said that the Universe knows the precise, perfect time for the cocoon to open up so that the young butterfly can spread its wings and fly away. According to him, it's the same with us. But, like the butterfly, we must be willing to wait.

Remember my Cherokee friend, Neal? The man of few words? He was telling me that there were three ways for us to purify ourselves. The first way was to find our Yes and our No inside us, and we'll talk about the third way later. The second way, according to him, called for us to create a special place in our homes where we can quiet our minds and let go of all the cares and worries of the day. He said that meditation purifies us, and it is best done in a comfortable place where we can be away from any of the noise and hubbub of the world.

"Is there anything else I need to take into consideration before I do this?" I asked him.

"No," he replied. "Just that thoughts and memories are stored in stone and bone and wood and fabric."

That made no sense at all to me. I started to ask him what he was talking about, but before I could speak, he went on. "It doesn't even have to be a place, my friend. It could be a straw mat you sit on, or a shawl that you wear around you. In fact, it doesn't really matter where or what it is," he said, "what matters is that you go there on a regular basis and commune with Spirit. As you do this over time, your special place or mat or shawl will begin to carry the subtle vibrations that you've established there, and they'll emanate the spiritual frequency you've created. That way, when you're feeling a little run down or overwhelmed by the cares of today's fast-paced world, you can go to your special place, or sit on your mat, or wrap your shawl around you, and it will give you a boost! Instead of having to wait for the feeling of Spirit to settle in, like you usually do, it'll be there almost immediately."

Two days later, I met a lady who mentioned that she sold shawls and, remembering Neal's advice, I bought a nice brown one. That was a while back, and nowadays I take it with me wherever I go. I can't explain it, but Neal was right. Whenever I put it on, I feel lighter right away.

*There are easier ways of doing things.*

Once you speak your intent,
set it free.
Let it go
so that Great Oneness Divine
and all the angelic helpers
can step in and work their magic.
Refrain from meddling and interference.
Do not dig up the little seedling
to see how it's doing.
Trust that it's in good hands.

We simplify our lives considerably
by cutting back
on the struggle and strife,
fret and worry—
first by intending,
then by trusting.
Let go of the doubtful voices
inside and out.
Ignore them
or command them: Be Gone.

Simplify

Then remain nonchalant
and know
to the depths of your Being
that your creation
is on its way to you.

Soon you gain confidence
that turns into courage
that becomes fortitude.
As you align with the Highest Good
you become like the mountain,
beautiful and immobile,
a fortress of strength.
This is how you manifest.

Creation is not meant to be hard,
but if you find it so,
start with small things —
parking places,
free tickets,
a friend to help you.
Be open to receive
from unexpected sources.

Be vigilant of your thoughts,
discard the ones
that would have you
distracted,
discounted,

doubtful,
or on a deadline.

Thank them and send them on their way.
You don't need them anymore.

If you really want to simplify your life,
give it all up to God
and trust in the dynamic dance
of the Highest Good.

That's the attitude that opens the way
for Great Oneness Divine
(which is the only Source there is)
to give it All up to you.

*The next time* *you make an intention—it doesn't matter what it is—resolve, at the same time, that you're willing to wait as long as it takes for it to manifest. Do this for a few of your intentions, then step back into a state of divine nonchalance, knowing that whatever you're intending is coming to you in its perfect timing. Now you're free to experience patience, and one of the first things you'll discover is that stress is not as much a part of your life as it once was. It's gone by the wayside because peace of mind has stepped in and taken its place.*

*In order to have it all*

*you've got to give it all up.*

# THE FIFTH INTENT
## STAY POSITIVE

*I see good, say good, and do good. I accept the gifts from
all of my experiences. I am living in grace and gratitude.
I stay positive.*

Some people just have a knack for manifesting. I met
Jennifer Olson in Vallejo, California, not long after I
left Hawaii. She came to one of my talks in the Bay
Area, and subsequently called me up because she wanted to
start an Intenders Circle in her home. Within two weeks, Jen
had gotten several of her friends together and, to make a long
story short, I became a regular at her circle, and we became
the best of friends.

During the period of time that I attended Jen's Intenders
Circle, I saw her manifest so many things that it gives me goose
bumps just to think about it. She intended and manifested
two houses, a motor home, a couple of cars, trips around the

country, and on and on. In fact, it was Jennifer who accompanied me to New Mexico where we both stepped into our greatest abundance—she with a fabulous home in the Red Rock country of Jemez Springs, and myself on an Arabian horse ranch in Corrales.

As I watched Jen create such a wonderful life for herself, I began to wonder what it was that made the difference between a mighty manifester like her and others who seemed to spend a lot of time in limbo, waiting for their intentions to manifest. The secret, I discovered, was staring me in the face all the time. Jen was a happy, positive person. She was always having fun. Life had blessed her with a great sense of humor, so much so that when someone asked her what she did for a living, she'd tell them she was a "certified laughing instructor." I even remember a couple of times in our Intenders Circles when she stood up, started patting her belly, said "Hah!" three or four times and, within a few seconds, the whole group was in stitches.

Jen and I now live several hundred miles apart, and we don't see as much of one another as we'd like, but I think of her often, and I'm especially reminded of an intention she made regularly in our circles: *"I intend that I always see good, say good, and do good."* It left such a strong impression on me that, even after I left New Mexico, I shared it with others as I traveled around the country. I figured, and rightly so, that if it worked so well for Jen, it would work just as well for the rest of us. As for myself, this simple intention constantly reminds me to stay positive. Whenever I'm feeling a little down or hear myself saying something that I really wouldn't want to manifest, I go back to Jen's intention to see good, say good, and do good, and everything just seems to get better from then on.

## ⸺ An Intenders Story ⸺

*We have a small group of friends who have made a very unusual agreement with each other. We get together every week or so for the sole purpose of socializing and keeping one another's words pure.*

*You see, about three years ago, we realized that our thoughts and our words are much more important than we had previously believed. We looked at our lives and found out that the experiences we were going through, and the beliefs that made us the way we are, resulted from something we'd said or thought. In other words, our words and thoughts were having a direct effect upon our future. With this in mind, we thought it would be wise to help each other use words that really served us and, likewise, gently let one another know when we were using words that weren't going to give us the results we desired.*

*We called it "conscious languaging" and, the more we learned about it, the more we noticed that the quality of our lives improved because we paid attention to it. I'll give you an example.*

*After we'd been meeting for a few weeks, we began to understand that the words we used to describe the same situations had completely different feelings about them. For instance, we noticed, at first, that we had a tendency to talk about our **problems**. In some ways, it helped us, but, overall, we observed that it usually didn't feel very good. That's when somebody said, "Well, let's not*

call them problems anymore. Let's call them **challenges** instead."
So we began to do this, and we really did start to feel more positive
toward these kinds of experiences. A challenge didn't feel the same
as a problem. It felt better. It seemed to weigh less heavily on us,
while subtly suggesting that we bring out our best and rise to the
occasion.

We went on like this for a while, replacing the word problem
with the word challenge when, one evening, we got to talking more
about it, and somebody said that we could even be more positive.
After all, when we resolved a challenge, we actually underwent a
transformation, a change that seemed to evolve us in some way. So,
from that point on, we decided to replace the word challenges with
the words **transformational opportunities**.

That worked well, but only for a short time. Perhaps because
it was so cumbersome to say, or because we'd started to look even
deeper into the subject of adversity, what our studies showed us was
that, when we overcame an adverse situation, we got stronger. Seen
from the positive side, our adversity became a blessing in disguise.
It became a **gift**.

So, in our quest to use words that serve us, we went from
**problems** to **challenges** to **transformational opportunities** to
**gifts**. We all agreed that these words can describe the same events,
but we are a lot more inclined to approach a situation where we'd
receive a gift than we are to face a problem. It just feels better that
way.

*Katie Myers*
*Pensacola, FL*

It's always been my intention to think and speak more positively, and yet there have been times when, for reasons I didn't understand, it seemed to be more difficult to keep my thoughts and words in a positive frame. One rainy spring afternoon as I was sitting in my small writer's cabin in Pagosa Springs, Colorado, I began to wonder what caused so many people, myself included, to be so readily inclined to entertain the negative side of things. It seemed to me as if our entire society is locked in the grasp of some dark force that rarely offers us a moment's rest from the negativity. Finally, in frustration, I decided to consult my inner guidance and see if I could get some answers.

I started out by taking a few deep breaths, then I said a short prayer invoking the Highest Good, closed my eyes, and did my best to quiet my mind. It wasn't but a minute before Lee Ching came in and started talking to me. Here's what he said:

*"Within your immediate surroundings are objects that are commonly called thoughtforms that act upon you in ways you do not presently perceive. If you could imagine yourself swimming through an endless, etheric substance, similar to the way a fish swims through the ocean, you would see all sorts of shapes that appear to have a life of their own. Each of these thoughtforms carries a specific message or a bit of information, and it is this information that can be helpful to you, or it can hinder your forward movement. Much depends on your level of awareness, for your mind is the receiver of the information carried by the thoughtforms, and to*

the extent that you are able to recognize certain thoughts as they come into your vicinity, you can either 'take them on' and become subjected to their influence, or you can deflect them and render them harmless.

Historically, over many hundreds of thousands of years, Beings from all across the cosmos have come to the Earth and planted, as well as maintained, certain thoughtforms in your world. Some of these Beings, like Jesus Christ and the Ascended Masters, have infused your world with thought forms of Love, mercy, and compassion, with the intention of helping you to achieve the highest experience available to you, which is to become one with God in this lifetime. Other Beings who have visited your Earth have also seeded your world with thoughtforms; however, these have not been beneficial to you. These Beings have literally fed themselves from your energy, like parasites or pirates, robbing you of your precious energy and taking it for their own selfish purposes. In order to do this, they have filled your etheric environment with negative thoughts designed to enslave you and keep you living at a low level of existence.

To extricate yourselves from these selfish influences, you must understand that you, as human Beings, are infinitely powerful in your own right. Your attention is of the utmost importance. Depending upon which thoughts you choose to put your attention on, and depending upon the words you speak, you can either give full expression to your power, or you can give it away. The Beings who would steal your energy are very adept at their deceptive practices. However, there is one vital piece of information that they have systematically withheld from you, and it is this: You manifest what you say you want, and you manifest what you say you don't want.

This means that, when you express yourself in a negative fashion, you draw the exact opposite of what you desire to yourself. An example of this is evident when you say that you don't want an accident or a sickness to occur. What most of you don't understand is that, by talking about anything—whether you want it or you don't—you invoke it; you attract it into your experience.

You see people do this all the time. They'll be talking about something they wouldn't want to happen, and, sure enough, it happens. What they weren't aware of is that, in their thinking processes, they pictured it happening. Since their thoughts are always creating their future, they, in fact, brought it to life when they said they didn't want it to happen.

Some thought forms are designed to play tricks on you, having you believe that you are keeping your undesired experiences at bay by voicing your resistance to them. Now, however, as you're beginning to explore more closely how your thinking works, you can see that you are undermining or sabotaging yourself by all your negative talk; that you are the cause of your calamities by virtue of the fact that you talk about them.

The antidote to having calamities and accidents befall you is to speak only in the positive, to be even more vigilant of what you're saying, and to stop yourself before you give voice to the negative. Then you can replace the 'I don't wants' and all the talk of calamities by saying what you do want. If, for instance, you catch yourself saying, 'I don't want war'—which, as you have learned, will only

*conjure up more aggression and violence—instead, you can say,*
*'I intend that I am living in peace.' As you phrase your words like*
*this, you invoke only the positive. There's no possibility for war*
*because you haven't mentioned anything about it.*

*Integrating positive languaging into your everyday vocabulary*
*may take a little bit of practice. As you become more aware of what*
*you are saying, your old negative habits will tend to surface, and*
*it will be common for you to have to take a few moments to figure*
*out the positive way to say something. This is the same as in your*
*Intenders Circles, where you have often had to help each other find a*
*positive way to phrase an intention. It is good that you have learned*
*to do this, because this exercise has helped you to become more posi-*
*tive people. You've begun to look upon these instances as an oppor-*
*tunity to sharpen your creative abilities. While you've found that*
*it's challenging at times to speak positively, you've also learned that*
*it can be fun. That's the spirit with which we in the higher realms*
*recommend you approach positive languaging. Make it fun.*

*After all, having fun is always a positive thing."*

When we have a thought
that isn't positive,
perhaps it makes us angry
or is limiting in some way.
We can choose another thought
that serves us better.

This requires vigilance.
We must watch our thoughts
closely

The Fifth Intent

and be willing
to make changes
in our ideas,
in our spoken words,
in our emotional investments.
For that which binds us to our old ways
is a thought form
hovering nearby
looking to make us angry
or sad.
Its justifications are endless.

To manifest our dreams
we must adhere to the Law
and remember:
Our thoughts are the forerunners
of our experiences.

Then look closer still
for the thought that works best:
the one that turns sad into happy,
anger into kindness,
scarcity into abundance,
irritation into peace,
hatred into love.

As we replace the negative with the positive
we see that the results
of having made this shift

Stay Positive

are filtering down
into our daily experiences
where we receive the gifts
we truly desire.

How often we jump to conclusions.
How often we sink into despair
out of habit.

Remember that all things can be seen
from a positive point of view.
All diseases
have been healed.
All people
deserve companionship.
All facets of the human condition
can be improved.

We are evolving
and getting excited now
because we see
that our challenges
are showing us something about ourselves
that we can change,
first by thinking it,
then by being it.

Know this:
It is within each of us

The Fifth Intent

to create our ideal
by starting from where we are in this moment
and expressing our gratitude
for all things.

We can change our thoughts
and change our lives
and change our world
by becoming perpetual optimists
and lifting our Spirits
to the heights.

*The first exercise here suggests that you catch yourself and set your intent before you give voice to your next complaint. **The next time** a dark thought comes in, immediately, without giving it the slightest chance to gain momentum, notice it, stop putting any more attention on it, and start thinking the exact opposite in whatever way feels appropriate to you. If it comes back again, treat it like an unwelcome guest, command it to go away, and then replace it with a thought you'd really like to see manifested in your life. Know that what you say is what you'll get. Your thoughts are the tickets to your happiness and all that you desire. But you must keep them positive if you're intending for your life to change for the better.*

*An additional exercise that is very helpful in these most fascinating of times asks you to "keep your eyes on the prize." **The next time** someone comes up and says that there could be a horrible cataclysm, you can respond by saying that you've recently realized that it's best for you to withdraw your attention from those* things because you don't want to be creating or reinforcing them. Instead, when they mention a potential catastrophe, you can talk about what you'd really like to be manifesting. You can share your vision of a better world. This posture allows you to hold a detached perspective when it comes to preparing for disaster. Of course, it's okay to keep an eye on the trends of the day and peek in at what humanity is collectively creating for itself. You may even want to move out to the country and become more self-sufficient, if that's where your interests lie. But it doesn't serve you to add to the creation of catastrophic events by becoming desperate or emotionally involved in them. Your job is to remain uplifted, to stay focused on "the prize," regardless of any chaos or negative hype that's running through the mainstream. By intending and completely trusting that you are guided, guarded, protected, and connected with the Highest Good in all situations, you'll find that you can walk through fire and be completely unaffected by it. You will observe and accept whatever is happening around you—without buying into anything or becoming emotionally overwhelmed—because you're creating something different. You're creating a peaceful, fulfilling environment for yourself.

*Misfortune is always accompanied by an incredible gift. Look for the gift and you will find it.*

# THE SIXTH INTENT
# SYNCHRONIZE

*After intending and surrendering, I take action by*
*following the opportunities that are presented to me.*
*I am in the flow where great mystery and Miracles abide,*
*fulfilling my desires, and doing what I came here to do.*
*I synchronize.*

I stepped into the flow of the miraculous when I let go of the mainstream. I can't tell you that it was a conscious decision on my part to live on the fringes of society. All I knew was that conforming to what everyone else was doing, residing in a crowded metropolitan area, going to a 9-to-5 job, and so forth didn't appeal to me anymore. I'd lost my interest for these things. At the same time, I was starting to see through the myriad illusions offered by the current educational, media, and governmental systems. As a result, I dropped out and moved to the country where, for the first time in my life, I could live in the hills, relatively free from the pressures of my peers to conform.

And free I was. I got up every morning and did what I wanted to do, all day long. It wasn't long before I discovered that, even if I didn't have any money, the Universe always provided for me. I never went hungry, nor was I wanting for anything, because I was free and following the flow of opportunities that life presented to me.

After twenty-five years of living a simpler lifestyle, stepping back into the mainstream was the furthest thing from my mind. There was no way I was going to do it. Not until . . .

*One night, after our Intenders Circle in Hilo, Lee Ching told me that I was going to be leaving my beautiful island home in Hawaii soon. He said that if I stayed there, my books would stay there with me. I had to take them out to the world if I was going to fulfill the plan I'd set for myself long, long ago.*

*Of course, I grumbled at first. I loved the islands; my land was paid for, and although I never had much money, my life as an avocado farmer was simple and free from a lot of complications. In short, I was no longer part of the workaday world and could have happily lived out the rest of my days in my coffee shack on the Big Island. But that isn't what happened.*

*The dynamics of how all this came about were as follows: I had gone to Reno to visit my mother over the Christmas holidays in 1997 and, while I was there, I rode the bus over to Petaluma, California, to take part in their new Intenders Circle. I received a warm welcome from Conrad and Gail and their friends, and when it came my turn to* say my intentions, I said, "I intend that I'm given a clear sign if I am to live here on 'the mainland.' I intend that I have a nice place to stay, and that it comes to me freely, easily, and effortlessly." Immediately, Gail and Johnna, who were later to become good friends, said they had an idea. Johnna had a spare room on her pygmy goat farm up on Sonoma Mountain, and I could stay there if I wanted to.

Well, that, to me, was as clear a sign as any. It made me feel so good that I decided to hang around Petaluma for a few days and, the next morning, I went to visit the goat farm, which turned out to be a lovely place. I couldn't wait to move in, but first I had to go back to Hawaii and get my belongings.

On the morning after I got back, I was taking a walk on the beautiful black sand at Kehena Beach on the eastern side of the Big Island and, on the spur of the moment, I took a copy of my novel, The Intenders of the Highest Good, set it on an outcropping of rocks above the high-tide line, blessed it, and offered it up to anyone who happened to find it. It was like a gift I was giving back to Mother Earth for all the help she'd given me recently.

A couple of weeks went by during which I took the rest of my money and bought a one-way, nonrefundable ticket to San Francisco, not having the slightest idea how I was going to get to Johnna's place when my plane arrived at 11 o'clock at night. Maybe I'd hitchhike. For years, I'd been hitchhiking around the Big Island, but little did I know that not too many people hitchhike around California these days, especially at 11 pm. Either way, I wasn't concerned, because I knew I was in a flow and that everything I needed would be taken care of. Lee Ching had told me that there were lots of people who were waiting to meet me once I got to the mainland.

And so I packed my backpack, one suitcase, and my old guitar and was ready to go when, two days before my flight was due to depart, I got a call from Johnna saying that she was very sorry but, due to circumstances she couldn't control, the room at her place on Sonoma Mountain was no longer available. I remember hanging up the phone and staring at the wall, thinking what the heck was I going to do now? That's when I heard Lee Ching's voice, as clear as day, inside my head. "You have to go," he said. "You have to get on that plane; there's no turning back now. Everything will be fine. Just trust, and see what happens."

Ironically, that night was my final Intenders Circle in Hawaii, and all my good friends showed up to wish me well and say their good-byes. It was a wonderful evening, full of joy and high spirits, and when it came my turn to say my intentions into the circle, I told them what had happened—that I'd just gotten a call that morning from Petaluma letting me know that the place I had counted on wasn't there anymore. And, on top of that, I had no transportation arranged for when I got there. Undaunted and trusting, I went ahead and stated my intentions anyway, saying, "I intend that I have a wonderful place to stay when I get to California, and that I have a nice vehicle of my own while I'm there."

Before I could say anything else, my best buddy, Mark, interrupted and asked me what kind of vehicle I would like. I said a van. I always liked vans. Then he interrupted again and said, "Well, what color?" To which I laughed and said, "Red! I intend I have a red van when I get to California."

We finished our intentions and toned, and it was as if the angels in Heaven sang with us that night. During our customary break before Tina was going to lead our weekly thirty-minute spiritual guidance session, a sparkling lady named Helen Noble pulled me aside and told me a very interesting story. She said that she'd been walking alone on Kehena Beach a couple of weeks earlier and had, to her great surprise, found a copy of my novel sitting on the lava rocks. She took it home and read it in two days. In fact, it was what prompted her to come to our Intenders Circle that evening. She went on to say that she enjoyed the book so much that she'd mailed it to her daughters, Nancy and Patti, who lived in Sonoma, California. That morning, she'd talked to them on the phone, and they'd both read it and said they'd like to meet the guy who wrote this book!

I'll never forget the feeling that swept over me when Helen asked if I'd like her to call them and see if they had a place for me to stay. I said, "That would be great," and she immediately walked over to the phone, made the call, and took care of everything. I even spoke to Patti, and she said they'd be glad to pick me up at the San Francisco airport at 11 o'clock at night.

But wait! That's not the end of the story. Two evenings later, I flew to California. Nancy and Patti picked me up as promised and, after stopping for a late-night snack at a Denny's near Sausalito, we drove into the quaint little town of Sonoma. Seeing how tired I was, Patti graciously put me in the back room, where I slept deeply for a few hours, only to be awakened early the next morning by a whole bunch of little children running around my bed. As it turned out, Patti ran a day-care center, and the kids, as cute and cuddly as they were, were not included as part of the environment I'd imagined for myself in California. You see, I'd been a hermit for the last twenty-five years, living a quiet, secluded life back in the hills of Hawaii. Not only that, but I was a writer, and writers, I told myself, needed silence to do their work. In short, I realized that I'd neglected to intend that I had a quiet place to live while I was on the mainland.

So, after a cup of coffee with Patti and Nancy, I called the only other person I knew in Sonoma, a lovely lady named Dottie who had come to our circle when she was on vacation in Hawaii a few months earlier. As it turned out, Dottie only lived three blocks away and she invited me to come over for a late breakfast. I walked over about 10 o'clock, just as her roommate, Betts, was getting ready to go out the door for her weekly meeting in the nearby town of Napa with a circle of friends who called themselves "The Voyagers." We chatted for a few minutes and, on the spur of the moment, Betts asked if I'd like to come along with her. I agreed, and we hopped in her car and drove through the beautiful, rolling hills and vineyards to the Unity Church in Napa. The Voyagers turned out to be a delightful group of about fifteen people, all over the age of seventy, who listened to inspiring, channeled tapes sent each week from Virginia Beach, and then said prayers into their circle. I told them about The Intenders and said that, if they didn't mind, I'd like to say some prayers with them, and say some intentions as well. They agreed and, when it was my turn, I started off by explaining that I had just arrived from Hawaii the night before, was staying in a day-care center, and I intended that I have a nice, quiet place to live while I'm here in California.

No sooner had I said "So be it" than the debonair man who was sitting on my right tugged on my sleeve and whispered that I could stay at his place for as long as I liked. Richard Robinson, who later turned out to be a very close friend and confidant, said that I could move in right away. So, when the meeting was over, Richard and I drove back through the vineyards to Sonoma where I picked up my backpack, suitcase, and guitar, thanked Patti and Nancy profusely, and headed back to Napa.

As we reached the edge of town, Richard pulled into a parking space in front of a hardware store and went in to get something. After a few minutes, he came out with a thin paper bag and, with my curiosity getting the best of me, I asked him what was in the bag. He explained as he drove that he had an older van for sale and that in the bag were a couple of For Sale signs. Right away, my wheels started turning. I only had $37 in my pocket; however, I was determined to trust that I was doing what I came here to do, that I was meeting the exact people I was supposed to meet, and that I was in a magical flow with the Universe taking care of everything. He described the van as a 1985 Toyota with just under 200,000 miles on it, and, with a sparkle in his eye, he said he wanted $2,000—a good price, considering that, like himself, it was in great shape for being that old.

As we rounded the corner and pulled into his driveway, there sat the van—but something was amiss. It wasn't red! It was silver! This couldn't possibly be my van. It was the wrong color. Besides, I reminded myself, I didn't have anywhere near $2,000.

Talking to myself the whole time, I got out of the car and went to grab my things from out of the trunk of Richard's car when he handed me the bag and asked if I wouldn't mind placing the For Sale signs in the windows of the van. I said I'd be happy to and, as I walked around to the far side and opened the passenger door to the van, my heart did a somersault. The interior of the van was RED!

To make an already long story short, two days later, Betts cosigned a note at the bank with me, and the van was mine!

We always took a few minutes for questions and answers at the end of our spiritual guidance sessions so that Lee Ching could help us with any personal challenges we had. It was during one of these sessions that I asked him how we could tell whether we were evolving or not. He responded by saying that each and every one of us came to this Earth with a plan for accomplishing a specific purpose while we are here. If all goes well, at a certain point in our lives, we rediscover our agenda and we align with it. I asked him what was the best way to do this, and he said that we can find out what our plan is by taking stock of what our desires are. If we have strong desires in one direction it means that, as we go about the business of fulfilling them, we are on our path. He explained further that our desires move us forward, that they're the signs we follow in order to make sure that we're doing what we came here to do.

The word *de-sire*, he said, comes from the Latin meaning "of the Father," and that, from a higher point of view, our desires come from our souls. We were born with them, and we evolve by either transmuting or fulfilling them.

The trick, he said, is, ultimately, to become desire-less. But how this plays out depends greatly on where we grow up. According to Lee Ching, if we were raised in one of the Eastern cultures, where meditation and solitude are common practices, we might retire to a monastery and meditate in order to transmute our desires. This works fine, he said. However, in the West, where consumerism is king, we're more apt to do things differently. What with all the advertising we've had thrown at us, the environment here isn't as conducive as it could be for us to transmute our desires. Instead, it's usually more appropriate for us to reach a state of desire-less-ness by fulfilling our material desires one by one until they're all satisfied. That way, we can become free of our desires and empowered at the same time.

Lee Ching also told us that another characteristic of our true paths is that they always have a spiritual aspect to them. We might spend years accumulating money and material goods, and he said that there's nothing wrong with that. But, eventually, we will have had enough of these things, and we'll look to explore ways to enrich our inner lives. Perhaps our characters will need fine-tuning; or we'll want to learn to act with more mercy, compassion, or kindness toward others. These are spiritual qualities, and here, in our Western culture, a great many of us only become interested in these pursuits after the bulk of our materialistic desires have been manifested. According to Lee Ching, unless we're born with a penchant for spiritual things, we typically become seekers only after we've acquired many of the things we always wanted.

*Anyone who desires to become more proficient at using the Intention Process must pass through six stages or steps before becoming an adept. I was fortunate to learn these steps from a tall, highly* intelligent man who mysteriously showed up at my doorstep one summer day when I was living in Corrales, New Mexico. He said his name was Ralph, and that he was an author of a different sort than I. Whereas I'd always been interested in the intuitive side of life, Ralph's talent, as I soon realized, was that he was scientifically oriented. He liked to analyze things and put them in order.

After a few minutes of customary introductions and niceties, we got to talking about the laws of manifestation, and Ralph said that, lately, he'd been writing about something he'd discovered in his research. It had to do with a particular progression that most people go through in order to become more skilled at manifesting.

The initial step in this progression, he said, was **testing**. If we're going to create anything consciously, we must first run a test by making an intention and establishing for ourselves that the process works. Once we realize that our intention has, in fact, manifested in our physical experience, we'll be more apt to test it again by making several more intentions and watching closely for them to manifest as well. In this way, he said, we gain a modicum of proficiency and work our way toward the second step in the progression: we begin to **trust**.

Ralph explained that, the more we see our intentions come into manifestation, the more our level of trust grows. We start to get comfortable with the process and, usually not long after that, we reach the third step, which he called **confidence**. Confidence, according to Ralph, comes to us when we understand that we're really on to something. At this point, we typically begin using the Intention Process more often. We use it to bring anything that we need into our lives, and we use it confidently.

After noticing that our intentions are coming to life on a steady basis, our confidence then turns into a **knowing**. This is the fourth step, and Ralph said that this is where our manifesting skills take a gigantic leap. He said that, in preparation for the book he was currently working on, he had interviewed hundreds of people and found that those who had a knowing about their ability to create consciously lived an altogether different kind of life from those who hadn't reached this stage yet. They had a charisma about them; they'd come in touch with their innate power, and, from this point on, there was no turning back. He said it was as if they'd awakened from a dream and had no desire to go back to sleep. Life had regained its excitement and adventure, now that they had accessed their true power. The only thing left for them to do after that was to act courageously. And that is the fifth step: **courage**.

When we reach the stage of courage in our evolution, we are no longer hampered by what others think or say about us. Fear and intimidation don't play the same roles in our lives as they used to. We call forth the Highest Good and make our intentions courageously, knowing that whatever we're intending is going to manifest for us.

Our base of power grows stronger and stronger, and soon, after acting with courage for a while, we reach the sixth and final level on our journey: **fortitude**. We become like a castle or an impenetrable fortress built upon the peak of the mountain. Having made our way through the previous five steps, we stand firm, at the pinnacle of life, masters of all we survey. Nothing can touch us now. We are grand creators, freed from all worldly cares as God's most precious gifts are arrayed before us to pick and choose from as we please.

If you're choosing to walk the path of empowerment, you'll need to get good at making your intentions, letting them go, and then taking action when opportunities present themselves. Taking action is where synchronicity comes in. If it's for your Highest Good, usually within a few days after you've surrendered your intentions up to the Universe, a series of almost surprising events will reveal themselves to you, and it is for you to move forward from one to the next until you reach your final goal. Suddenly, you'll notice that you're in a serendipitous flow where all good things are coming to you and that everything you need is magically there for you when you need it. From then on, all you have to do is stay alert to that which is in front of you until, one day, Great Mystery opens her arms wide in the form of a feeling you've rarely experienced and probably forgotten about. Your innocence will return, and life—the life you were truly meant to live— becomes an adventure once again.

To join the flow
you must let go
and be still
long enough
for a change to take place
inside of you.

The clamoring of your thoughts
does not disturb you now.
Your memories of the past

take their rightful place
among your other useful tools.
Your expectations of the future
are also put aside.
Now you are free to cross the threshold
that stands at the entrance
to your feelings.
Your mind will only take you so far
with its analyzing and anticipating.
It will not put you in touch with Great Oneness.

But here, in the center of your feelings,
you will find your intuition,
your power,
your femininity,
your magic,
your Mother
awaiting your approach.

As you take action
and move forward
in the direction of your dreams,
She will guide you
and enlist her legions of helpers
to show you the way
when you are lost,
to present opportunities
when you are stuck,

Synchronize

to reveal your calling
when you are ready.

She sends her hawks and her crows,
her dolphins and her whales,
her cats and her dogs,
her Sun and her winds,
her rainbows and her sparkling reflections,
her signs within signs.
They may surprise you
but you will know them,
and if you follow them,
they will take you home.

*The next time* *you're sitting in a quiet place out in Nature (or on your back porch), let all of the cares and worries of life go for a short time. Breathe deeply, and then, when you're ready, call forth the Highest Good and intend that your next step, the one that places you firmly upon your soul's path, is revealed to you. Intend that any signs or intuitive hunches that will make it easier for you to recognize your path are given in such a way as to be unmistakable to you. Intend, too, that you are guided, guarded, and protected every step of the way—and then go about your day. From this point on, all you have to do is wait and be ready for an opening. It won't take long. An old acquaintance will show up who needs your help. Or a new offer will bring unexpected opportunities your way. Or perhaps it may even be that a beautiful bird or a beam of sunlight through the trees will set you in the right direction.*

The Sixth Intent

The important thing is that you follow it, because once you do, so much more will avail itself to you.

Though you have asked
for that which you have desired,
there is so much more
that is awaiting to be given you.

# THE SEVENTH INTENT
# SERVE OTHERS

*I practice love in action. I always have enough to spare and enough to share. I am available to help those who need it. I serve others.*

In the autumn of 2003, I received a call from a pleasant-sounding lady in Canada named Rebecca. She'd heard about my work and wanted to know if I'd be interested in coming up to give seven workshops, seven nights in a row, each in a different location around Vancouver Island. Her best estimates were that we would attract a minimum of 100 people each night, because she was in the promotion business and she would take care of everything. All I had to do was show up.

Well, this, I must tell you, was the best news I could possibly have received, the very break I'd been waiting for. You see, I'd been writing books for several years, but had never really made it into a larger market like my inner guidance said I would. I kept moving forward because I knew my books were helping people, and I'd received an abundance of emails and letters complimenting my work. I was sure my time would come. It just hadn't come yet.

Another factor in all of this was that I was having to integrate my own teachings into my life at this time, which meant that I was trusting that I'd have everything I'd need to fulfill the task I'd set for myself in the exact moment I needed it. My schedule required me to write every day, so I didn't want to tie myself down with a regular job; instead I'd have to count on small jobs and whatever came in from the sale of my books from The Intenders Web site to get me by. I was well aware that this was not a "secure" way of life, but it did allow me to put my manifesting and level of trust to the test.

I was living in southern California at the time, but, from the minute I arrived there, I was faced with another kind of shock. San Diego was more crowded and more frenetic than anywhere I'd ever been. I wasn't prepared for the big city. Everything was hard for me there. I was always on the edge financially and, several times, I remember entirely forgetting my own teachings and grumbling about how I'd lost my touch at manifesting. To this day, I'm not sure why I was there. I can only suppose that I needed to experience, firsthand, how people in the city survived. After all, how was I going to be able to write books that were meant to help the people there if I wasn't able to identify with what they were going through?

Most of the folks I met in the city were very friendly but stressed out, going from paycheck to paycheck and stuck in a cycle that they couldn't get out of. The rent had to be paid, so they had to have a job, had to have a car, had to have insurance, had to have a phone, and so forth. They had to have have have, so they could go go go, and do do do. A lot of them appeared to be compromising on a moment-to-moment basis, doing all sorts of things they didn't really want to do in order to pay the monthly bills. I also noticed that there was an undercurrent of fear that seemed to permeate the whole city, and I attributed this to the ever-worsening conditions of overpopulation that existed there. Needless to say, for someone who'd lived most of his adult life out in the country, it wasn't the right place for me.

So when I got the call from Rebecca, I couldn't say "yes" fast enough. Immediately, my mind went to work on the math . . . Seven nights at 100 people per night at $20 each equaled around $14,000. Add another $6,000 for book and video sales, and I'd come home with around $20,000 in my pocket. Considering that I only had $12 to my name at the time, this sounded pretty good to me. I'd have to borrow $300 for the trip, but that didn't matter because when I got home I'd have all the money I needed to reprint my dwindling supply of Intenders Handbooks and pay off every debt I had.

When it came time to go, I called my good friend and fellow Intender Adrian Ulrey in Oceano and arranged to stay at her place on my first night on the road. Adrian and I were kin from way back, and I couldn't wait to see her again, but when I got there, she didn't act at all like the bright and shining Adrian I'd come to know. I asked her what was going on. In a hushed voice, she said that the doctors were checking her out.

In fact, she had an appointment in the nearby town of Solvang in less than an hour—would I mind driving her there? I gladly agreed since I wanted to be with her as much as possible.

When she stepped out of the doctor's office, her face was ashen white, her whole aura turned dull. I hugged her and asked what happened. As it turned out, the doctor told her the worst thing that anyone could possibly imagine. According to him, she had two months left to live.

We drove home and I remember holding her hand the whole way. She said that she didn't know what to do, that she had three daughters living within an hour's drive, but, because of their jobs, they were too busy to stay with her full time. We cried, made some intentions together, and, unbelievably, by dinnertime she'd bounced back slightly.

That night, after dinner, I decided to call Rebecca and check in. Little did I know that I was about to get my second major shock of the day. Rebecca apologized for not getting back to me sooner, and said that she really hadn't had time to arrange things properly, so the reservations weren't coming in as she'd expected. In other words, my series of workshops— my ticket to success—was canceled. I explained to her that I was already partway there, and that I'd borrowed $300 for the trip, but all she could do was say she was sorry.

I was sitting out on Adrian's back porch at the time, thinking, on one hand, that my dreams of financial success had vanished before my eyes and, on the other hand, that my good friend Adrian needed help. The Universe seemed to be trying to tell me something.

I went inside and told Adrian about my conversation with Rebecca and asked her, at the same time, if she'd like me to stay and take care of her for as long as I was needed. Well, she instantly lit up like a Christmas tree! In fact, I lit up too because, in that moment, I knew that I was exactly where I was supposed to be, doing exactly what I was supposed to be doing. Nothing ever felt more right, and I told Adrian so.

The next two months—she passed away exactly sixty days to the day of her diagnosis—were a true joy for me. Adrian, throughout the whole process, was a pillar of courage and strength, never complaining once, never taking one pain-killer, always grateful for every moment of her life. We read the *Course in Miracles* every evening and talked until late into the night about Spirit. I learned things about life and death I never would have learned unless I'd spent this time with Adrian. I was especially grateful that I was given the opportunity to be with her the moment she died. I'd never done anything like that before and, let me tell you, it was a true blessing and an honor to have been there. The only way I can describe it is to say that it felt like we were surrounded by God's holiest angels throughout the entire evening.

Looking back, I wouldn't have traded my experiences in Oceano for anything. The Universe had delivered me to Adrian's house by tempting me with riches and success, but that isn't what I got. I got so much more. I learned that, when I serve a friend, I'm really serving myself.

When I got back to San Diego after Adrian's passing, I checked in with Lee Ching and asked him about my experiences in Oceano. He said that my angels had tricked me, for my own good, into staying with Adrian so I could learn how to serve others better. He also said that, previously, I hadn't been available enough to serve others in a way that really helped them. As with most people, money, or the lack of it, had been a stumbling block to my serving effectively. But, according to him, it didn't need to be that way.

He went on to say that one of the biggest blocks to our being available to serve others is our attitude of hoarding. Most people don't realize it, but hoarding always shuts down the flow of our abundance, while giving always comes back to us in great measure. The mechanics of this phenomenon are easily apparent once we get past our old attitudes about "saving for a rainy day." It works like this: when we hoard something, whether it's our money, our time, our resources, or our energy, we're actually doing it because we've pictured ourselves in a situation where we've run out of things. We've envisioned ourselves down and out, perhaps even destitute and depressed. Now, this vision is a thought, and it will work its way into physical manifestation just like any other thought we keep our attention on. In other words, by saving for a rainy day, even though our motivation is to have extra resources for later on, we sabotage our future and create the exact opposite of that which we truly desire for ourselves.

If we're really going to be able to serve others, he said, it furthers us to bring our limiting thoughts to light so that we can replace them with thoughts that will bring our abundance to us. There's a good example of this, he said, in how the kitchen faucet works. When we open the valve, the water comes in and the water goes out. But when we close off the valve, the water can't come in because it is not flowing out. It's the same with our money and our resources; we close off the flow of all good things coming to us by our thoughts of lack and our subsequent acts of hoarding. By the same token, we open the faucet of our abundance and keep it open by spending, not frivolously, but responsibly. When we spend without worrying about it, we send a message to the Universe that we have enough of everything we need, and that we trust that there will always be more when we need it. It's this posture that delivers our abundance to us (if it's for our Highest Good), and provides us with enough to spare and enough to share, so that we'll be able to serve others in the way we'd want ourselves to be served.

*There was something else that happened while I was at Adrian's that made a big impression on me. One morning as I was walking on Grover Beach, I made an intention to learn how to be of better service to others and, within a couple of weeks, I met Patty. To this day, I don't even know her last name or anything else about her, except that she was from Bakersfield. This is how it happened. A few days after her seventieth birthday, when Adrian "changed address" (that's what we called it in Hawaii), her daughter, Annie, called their mutual friend, Patty, to let her know about it. Patty immediately got in the car and drove for two hours to Oceano where the family was gathering.*

*Though quiet and unpretentious, Patty walked in the door and wasted no time asking what she could do. Did someone need a ride to the store? Was there anything that anyone needed? Annie said that her mother's wishes were to remain in the house for the next seventy-two hours, and that we would need some ice to keep Adrian's body from decaying too rapidly. Patty volunteered and left right away to go get it. When she returned, she asked again how she could be of help. Were there other family and friends to be notified? Annie agreed that that was a good idea, so Patty immediately started compiling a list and making phone calls.*

*Over the next several days, Patty was always helping. It didn't matter what needed to be done or who she had to do it with, she just did it. Cooking, cleaning, sweeping, you name it. Sometime late on the second day of working with her, something clicked within me. Right there in front of me was the answer to my intention—the embodiment of the true spirit of service—Patty! She was always looking for ways to help others. For her, it was an ongoing thing. She didn't want any money, nor was she religious (or if she was, she never mentioned it). She just wanted to help, and nothing else seemed to matter.*

*Looking back, I'm not sure if she even knew what she'd taught me by her shining example. But, no doubt, that wouldn't have mattered to her either.*


As we shift into the new paradigm and move away from an attitude of service to self to one of service to others, we'll each, in our own way, come to a point when we realize that service to others is service to self. This usually happens when we get a glimpse of what our world would be like if everyone were serving everyone else. It's easy to see that we would all be much happier, more abundant, and less fearful if we were all serving each other. War, poverty, unrest, starvation, and the like wouldn't exist because we wouldn't allow our brothers and sisters to suffer like we do nowadays. We'd be helping them instead.

From one perspective, the roots of our current chaos lie in the political ideologies we cherish so much. We've been so indoctrinated by suggestions that ask us to side with one ideology or another—be it capitalism, communism, socialism, or anti-terrorism—that we've lost sight of the fact that none of them really work on our behalf. Indeed, what good can come from a system that encourages one person's profit at the expense of another's loss? That's the foundation upon which capitalism, the ideology of the West, is built. Profit and *loss*. Sure, it's given lots of Americans access to seemingly unlimited consumer goods, but when you look around the planet, large numbers of people are left out in the cold while we continue to bask in luxury.

Communism and the other "isms" are no better. They offer nothing more than the enslavement of the masses by the few in power and, unfortunately, those few have rarely shown any inclination to be benevolent toward those they represent.

Fortunately, there is one ideology that has the potential to deliver us from our current chaos and confusion, but it is seldom considered. It's called Love, and the only reason we don't drop all of the other ideologies and adopt it immediately is because it would disrupt the long-standing agendas of the power elite. Those who are in power believe that the only way they can stay in power is by propagating fear and suffering, by dividing and conquering. They never stop to consider that Love and all of its attributes—compassion, mercy, kindness, respect, honesty, forgiveness—would straighten everything out in a jiffy. Not to worry, however. They'll figure it out one of these days and, in the meantime, we can set an example for them.

## — An Intenders Story —

*It seems to me that one of the biggest barriers to really being of service to others lies in our tendency to "dumb down." You know what dumbing down is, right? Dumbing down is when we act like we don't know what's going on because we're afraid of others who appear to be more powerful than we are. It's when we're timid and don't say anything at times when we actually could have a positive influence on the situation. That's what I was doing.*

*I remember one specific time when I was sitting in a coffee shop with a group of friends, and one guy was saying that there really isn't any such thing as God, and that this reality here on Earth is the only one there is. This man was very strong willed, and I didn't say anything. I dumbed down, even though I'd had several mystical experiences and I **knew** that God exists.*

*Later on, after I got home, I thought about what we'd talked about, and something didn't feel right. There were several young people there that day and they were starting to believe the fellow who was so powerful. I could have served them by saying something to balance out his persuasive, but misguided, views. But I* didn't. So I intended, right then and there, that I would never miss an opportunity like that again.

Since then, I've come to understand that it doesn't serve anyone if I allow others to have their way just because they're more eloquent or more persistent than I am. I speak my truth, and now people don't run over me like they used to. My life, on a personal level, works so much better now that I've stopped dumbing down. Come to think of it, I'll bet our whole world would be better place if more of us would stop dumbing down and speak out for what we truly believe in.

Marcus Carroll
New York City, NY

## — An Intenders Story —

When I first decided to serve others, I didn't realize that it also included forgiving them. I thought I would help them out by cleaning or running errands or doing whatever they wanted, but what I came to understand was that I could help them in other ways as well.

The instance that brought all of this home to me was when I made an intention to help my aging mother. In 1998, I gave up my own apartment, moved in with my mom, and began to prepare her food, bathe her, and do all of the things necessary to make her last days as comfortable as possible. Up until then, I really hadn't made much of an effort to get close to her. She lived three states away, and we really didn't get along all that well anyway. In truth, there were long periods of time when we never spoke at all because I was still carrying a lot of anger toward her for things she'd done to me as a child. Mainly, I never understood how she could just stand by and let my father abuse me like he did.

But in the last few weeks of her life, as she lay in her deathbed with me sitting in the chair beside her, we began to talk about some of the things that we might not have otherwise spoken about. One particular evening after we finished eating and our barriers were lower than usual, I asked her why she let my dad beat me without ever coming to my rescue. Her answer showed me a side of her I never knew existed.

She explained that she had been just as afraid of him as I was, that he beat her and threatened her too, and that he was always very careful not to let anyone else know about it. She was so sorry, she said, but at the time she was totally incapable of giving me the love I needed because she was in fear for her own safety.

She started to cry when she told me the details. I felt such compassion for her, lying there in her bed like that, waiting to die any day. But, most of all, I felt sorry because we'd never talked like this before. When her tears stopped, and as I was wiping them from her cheeks, she touched my arm with her frail hand and asked me to forgive her for not being a good mother. She said she really loved me, both then and now, and that it would mean a lot to her if I could find forgiveness in my heart for her.

I didn't move except to brush away the tears from my own eyes. Suddenly, a very emotional experience when I was a teenager came to mind. My mother was in a bad mood and had punished me for something I was innocent of. It was in that moment that I decided, *resolutely, to put her out of my life. Now, however, as I recalled that highly charged event, I was able to see the unhappiness in her face that I hadn't seen before. I never knew she was that unhappy.*

*As my vision of the past receded, she looked up at me from her bed, our eyes met, and I told her that I forgave her, not just for that instance, but for everything uncaring she'd ever done to me. Then I leaned down to hug her and, as I did, it felt like a great weight was lifted from my chest. We both wept some more that night and, after that, something shifted in me . . . and in her. From then on, until the time she passed away, she was much calmer and at peace. The way I see it, our forgiveness healed us both.*

*Alan Matousek*
*Birmingham, AL*

So how do we create a better world? We begin, one on one, by helping each other. Or we start with a small group of friends dedicated to practicing Love in action, and we set an example for those around us. Love, you see, is contagious. When you notice someone helping someone else and making a big difference in their life, it makes you want to help someone else yourself. That's what the saints and those whom we admire most in our world have done. They've let go of their inclination to put themselves first and opted, instead, to see what happened when they served others. These people, not the power elite, are the true humanitarians and heroes of our time. They're the ones who hold the light for us when times are hard. And it is they, not the politicians, whom we should venerate and support.

Clearly, our current ideologies are passing away. Our civilization is falling apart, and with each passing day, our Spirit calls out to us from within. Its messages speak of an honoring that is taking place, first in small circles of people, then, soon, in the great masses. We are all learning, each in our own way, that when we honor and respect the Spirit of another, we move all of us closer to the highest of experiences. We move all of us, including the few power elitists, one step closer to God.

We can always find someone to help—
elderly people,
sick people,
children,
people with a dream.
Everyone needs help
at one time or another.

But we get too busy
and too distracted
by our worldly agendas,
by our next destination,
by our past problems.
We think we don't have time
to help someone else.

Amid the chaos
we have lost touch
with the treasures and rewards

The Seventh Intent

that come from serving others.
In our haste
we've missed an opportunity
to have an exquisite feeling
come over us,
a feeling that is gifted
to those who serve others
unconditionally.

You may make a lot of money
and travel to faraway places
or visit with famous people,
but the feeling that you get
from helping someone else
who really needs it
is like no other.
It will elude you, however,
until you stop
and make yourself available.
Then, someone will appear
who needs something
only you can give
and two things will happen:
they will be helped
and you will feel
the Love
that comes from loving,
the gift

Serve Others

that comes from giving,
and the harvest that comes from sowing
the seeds of kindness.

Ironies abound
when you go to help others.
Often the person who is being served
is not the one being helped the most.
But the one who is serving
unknowingly
derives the greatest benefit
from the encounter.

Along your journey
you will also need to discern
between one who really needs your help
and someone else
whose plans are selfish.
Sometimes it gets sticky
and you will be called upon to choose.
But if you ask for guidance
and call forth the Highest Good,
you will know what to do.

Before anything can happen, however,
the door that leads to Great Oneness
must be opened
by taking the first step
and making yourself available.

The Seventh Intent

One thing is certain.
If you intend to have someone to Love,
someone will come to you

There is no shortage
of people to Love.

*The next exercise is short and simple.* **The next time** *you see some-one who needs help, drop what you're doing and help them. Even if you're in the middle of something that seems very important to you, set it aside temporarily and be of service. It doesn't matter whether you know them or not, or even if you like them. Just help them out, and see what happens.*

*There are enough resources
on the planet right now
for the whole world to be fed and cared for.*

# THE EIGHTH INTENT
# SHINE YOUR LIGHT

*I am a magnificent being, awakening to my highest potential. I express myself with joy, smiling easily and laughing often. I shine my light.*

One of my first intentions upon arriving on the West Coast was to cultivate as many relationships with the clearest "channels" there as possible. To me, these are the people who have their hands on the pulse of the times we are living in. They best exemplify all that is coming to each and every one of us—namely, a connection with higher powers, angelic Beings, and/or invisible helpers seeking to guide us as we ring in a golden era.

Within two weeks, I met Jason Starkes through our mutual friend, Richard Robinson, in Napa, California. Jason is a thin, friendly, very charismatic man whose smile lights up the whole room. Richard had invited me to go with him to one of Jason's Wednesday-evening sessions, where about twenty people were gathered. Right off the bat, I was so impressed by Jason and his invisible colleagues, whom he called "The Nine," that, for the several weeks I lived in the area, I always went to hear what "The Nine" had to say. Jason and I became friends and, toward the end of my stay in Napa, he mentioned that he was going to present a workshop on the subject of abundance soon and asked me if I would like to attend.

Unfortunately, a couple of barriers stood between me and going to the workshop. First, I had no extra money at the time—the price tag for the workshop was around $200; second, I'd never gone to anyone else's workshops before. My ego, which was alive and kicking as usual, was very persuasive in proclaiming that I had no need of looking for information from others. After all, I was giving workshops of my own. Why in the world would I want to attend someone else's presentation?

As it turned out, I was chatting with Jason after one of his weekly sessions and, as if he knew what I was thinking, he said two things that immediately rid me of all my resistance. First, he said, "Tony, the teachers need the teachers." Well, the more I thought about it, the more I realized that what he said was true. How would I ever have gotten to where I was without B.J., Tina, Lee Ching, and all the others who'd helped me along the way? And second, he mentioned casually that, if money was a factor, I could pay him later, or not at all. Like me, he didn't want to keep people away from his workshops just because they didn't have the ready cash.

So one bright Saturday morning, I drove from the place I was staying in Napa to Rohnert Park where the workshop was being held and, within an hour, I knew I was supposed to be there.

After a brief introductory statement, Jason singled me out by asking me, point blank, what I thought was keeping me from my abundance. I said I had no idea. Then, for reasons I couldn't fathom at the time, he asked me about my paternal grandmother. What kept her from doing what she really wanted to do with her life?

I thought about it for a moment. I didn't know much about my grandmother on my father's side—just that, when I was very young, my mom and dad drove us all the way across the country to visit my grandparents and my grandmother, who was an extremely short, hunchbacked woman in her mid seventies, played the piano for us several times while we were there.

Jason prompted me again, asking what my grandmother's dreams were. This immediately brought back memories of a story my mother told me when I was a little boy. She said that Nana (that's what we called my grandmother) wanted desperately to be a concert pianist; her whole focus in life, until she met my grandfather, revolved around music. When she married my grandfather, however, all of her dreams were set aside in favor of more pressing matters. They had to make a living. He sold furniture in Chicago and later in San Leandro, California, and, luckily for me, she began having children.

As the years went by and the mundane tasks of life took over, the piano was all but forgotten. In sum, she never got to do what she really wanted to do.

I related this story to Jason and the others who sat around me in the workshop, and the room went quiet because it was a sad account of a life not lived to its fullest, of unrealized aspirations. When I said that my grandfather was a hardened, domineering man who had no intention of helping his wife do what she loved to do, the room went quieter still.

After a moment, Jason began to explain that, when my grandmother got to the point in her life when she knew she wasn't ever going to be a concert pianist, she transferred her dream to her eldest son, my father. According to Jason, if she couldn't create her own ideal life for herself, then she would do her best to see to it that my father was a success—*by her standards*. She would realize her dreams vicariously, through him.

I hadn't ever thought about it that way before. My first inclination was to wonder how "The Nine" knew so much about me. Surely, these were some of the most insightful observations I'd ever run across.

Next, to my surprise, Jason shifted gears and asked me what my father's dreams were. What did he really want to do with his life? Well, I knew a lot more about my father than I did about my grandmother, so this was easier. I remember one day when he and I were driving to the golf course after he'd gotten off work. He was a small-town doctor, a physician and surgeon, but he was also a very temperamental man. It didn't seem as if he really liked what he was doing. So I asked him what, when he was my age, he had wanted to be when he grew up. He said he wanted to be a tennis pro, that he dearly loved the game of tennis and was quite good at it, but that his mother had other ideas. She wanted him to be a successful doctor, no matter the cost. His tennis playing would have to go on the back burner while all of his studies, residencies, and internships were given their due.

Over the years, he quit tennis entirely and replaced it with the less strenuous game of golf, but this was only a hobby for him, a way to work off the tension of seeing sick people all day long.

I related this to Jason, and he said that, like my grandmother, my father wasn't able to live out his true dreams because other people had plans for him. Just as my grandfather derailed my grandmother's aspirations as a pianist, my grandmother, in her desire to have my father be the success that she wasn't, derailed his ambitions of being a tennis star.

It was a heart-wrenching story, but it made sense. Nobody in my family ever realized their dreams because someone else always had other plans for them. According to Jason, my grandmother wasn't the first in our family to follow this pattern; this thread ran through my entire ancestral lineage, going back for centuries, while not one person had ever done what they really wanted to do.

I was thinking that these were people's lives we were talking about, how their hopes and dreams seemed to mean nothing to those who supposedly loved them very much. That's when Jason looked straight into my eyes and said that this pattern had been passed down to me, that I was the seventh son of the seventh son, and it was up to me to cut the thread by taking a firm hold on my freedom and not acquiescing or allowing anyone else to tell me what to do. Then he asked me, very directly, what my dreams were. What made my heart sing?

I said I had several dreams. I wanted—intended—that I am writing books and giving workshops that make a difference in people's lives. I intended that I am making Mother Earth a cleaner, safer, more beautiful place to live. And I intended to know God in this lifetime and ascend.

Jason's response was that that was all possible, but first I'd have to free myself from the intentions and unconscious behavior patterns of my ancestors. I'd have to set my course for freedom and abundance, he said, because I can have it all.

The rest of the people in the room remained silent throughout our conversation, enthralled by the story that was unfolding. They knew that what he was telling me pertained to them as well, that we are all the seventh sons and daughters of our lineage, and it is up to us, in this generation, to live out our dreams.

And that's the moral of the story, thanks to Jason Starkes. We are the ones who must step forward, with courage and dignity, and set our course for freedom and abundance. We must come to understand, each in our own way, that we didn't come here to be enslaved, or to live under a dark cloud of debt, or do the bidding of those who came before us. Freedom— true freedom and the abundance that goes along with it—is as close as our next thought. It's time, now, for all of us who long to experience our highest calling to reach out for it, to grab hold with all our strength, and to cherish it for the gift that it truly is.

The Eighth Intent

It's unfortunate that so many people in our world today have allowed their lights to dim because they are unwilling to cut the threads between themselves and others who don't really care about them. Perhaps the most tenacious thread we'll need to cut if we're going to reclaim our power is the one that connects us to the moneylenders. This dark cord was originally created when we allowed our happiness to be tied to our bank accounts. You see, when the money is flowing and there's an abundance of it, as in the 1970s, we tend to be happy and express ourselves expansively. But when the flow of money has been restricted and we don't have as much of it as we'd like, then we begin to complain and withdraw from life, or struggle all the harder and stress ourselves out.

For those of us who don't have as much money as we used to and are feeling disempowered, here's a way to look at this dilemma so that we can begin to shine our lights again, regardless of how much money is in our pocketbooks.

First and foremost, we need to understand that our money really isn't worth anything. It's no longer backed by gold, silver, fine jewels, or anything at all. This means that, when we want to take out a loan from the moneylender, the most common exchange that takes place has us agreeing to work diligently in order to generate a regular monthly income for up to thirty years, while all the moneylender does is tap a few keys on his computer keyboard. No gold is moved, no work is produced on his part beyond the shuffling of a few papers. When it's over, the banker has another cup of coffee, while you walk out the door indentured, like a slave to the lord of the land.

The point is that there is a great imbalance in today's system. The banker does less than a half an hour's work at his desk, while you obligate yourself for a lifetime. Now, there's one more thing to understand: the biggest bankers are the ones who print and distribute the money, so they directly control how much of it we have, and how much it is worth in the marketplace. Indeed, they regulate the supply of money and can do anything they want with it, including persuading lawmakers to increase late fees, shorten payment periods, tack on more interest, etc. The fine print seems to get finer and harder to read with each passing day, as usury—which is the making of money from money without any other expenditure of energy—runs rampant across the land. No civilization in the history of mankind has lasted long when usury flourished. In fact, the more usury is allowed to proliferate in a society, the more that society decays and moves toward self-destruction. That's what we're witnessing in our world today. The current economic system doesn't work except for short periods of time, because there will always be someone who starts capitalizing on someone else's loss. In short, the moneylenders really aren't nice guys who have our best interests at heart. Their highest priority is to fill their own pockets with more money, with little or no feeling for how they're affecting us.

Here's the rub: subtly embedded within the structure of indebtedness lies a low self-esteem factor. We've been taught, primarily through the TV, that we should feel like we've done something very wrong when we're unable to make a payment on time. The moneylenders would relegate us to the position of second-class citizens for the sake of a few dollars or being a few days overdue. The letters that arrive from the bank in times like these are heartless and uncaring. Not only do they tack on surcharges, but they're also subliminally undermining our dignity.

And so, isn't it time we cut the threads between us and the moneylenders? Our present system isn't serving us anymore and we need to start over with a new system of money, one that's backed by something of worth and administrated only by those who have an unwavering conscience. The only question is whether we can make the transition smooth for ourselves, not only in our external world, but inside of us as well. Outwardly, we will need to barter, trade, reacquaint ourselves with our neighbors, and begin to help each other as much as we can during the transition. Of course, we will also need to cut the dark cord between us and the moneylenders, but even more than that, we will need to sever the connection between our happiness and our money. The wisest attitude to take is that we are happy if we have money, and we are just as happy if we don't have any money.

The best way to rid ourselves, once and for all, of our present money system is simply to forgive all debts everywhere, wipe the slate clean, and start over. Once the current usury and money-lending system goes away and is replaced by an equitable, honorable system of exchange, our lights will begin to shine brighter than ever before. It will be like stepping out of a dark prison cell into the light of a new day where all things are possible.

Shining our light implies that we give full expression to our lives, that we are so happy and carefree that we hold nothing back. Like small children, we show the world our true selves, vulnerably, trusting that, as long as we don't harm anyone, we can do whatever we want, go anywhere we want, be anything we want to be. This is the ideal. This is what most of us aspire to create for ourselves.

Can we have it all? Absolutely! Is there anything that can stop us? Only if we allow ourselves to be encumbered in any way. For it's the encumbrances—*the sapping of our energy by others who do not want us to be free to command and control our own energy and use it as we see fit*—that keep us from expressing ourselves fully. If we're going to shine our light, we'll need all the energy we can get. This means that, along with saying our intentions daily, we'll also need to cut the cords between us and all of our old, outdated beliefs, as well as the people who are propagating them. And for that, we'll want to learn to work directly with light.

*According to my Cherokee friend, Neal, the third way to purify ourselves is to envision a cascade of crystal-white light, like a waterfall, showering down upon us from above.*

*"In the old days," he said, "we used to imagine things like this, and if we were sick or blocked or had pain somewhere in our bodies, we would direct the light that came from the waterfall into the area that was afflicted. That's how we tried to heal ourselves."*

*He shook his head a little. "But that didn't work as well as we would have liked. We still had a lot of good people who didn't get* well. So we started looking more deeply into it and, after a while, we ran across something that completely revolutionized the way we approached our healing work."

"And what was that?" I asked him enthusiastically.

"We realized," he said, "that whenever we directed the healing light energy toward a particular area that we thought was afflicted, we would have to envision the blockage or resistance first. From that point, it didn't take us long to figure out that we really didn't want to be doing that, because it subtly reinforced the affliction."

He stopped talking and let that settle in for a moment, then he continued. "Since we knew that our thoughts were creating our reality, we didn't want our thoughts to be creating something that was causing us more pain . . . so this is what we did. We started envisioning the waterfall of light coming down from above us, surrounding and infusing every cell in our entire bodies with soothing blue-white light. That's all we did; we stopped envisioning the blockages. We simply pictured our whole bodies happy, healthy, and humming with light. That's what makes our Spirit shine, and that's what worked."

Did you ever sit down and consciously work with light, like the cascading waterfall that Neal describes? Working with the light is what allows us to transmute many of our old ways of doing things and go directly to that which we desire. Just like little children making castles in a sandbox, we can shape the light into anything we choose. Our imagination is the box, and light is the sand we use to create pictures in our minds that will, very soon, work their way outward into our physical world. It isn't complicated. In fact, we've been doing it all along. It's just that now we're learning to do it consciously. We're learning to do it so that it benefits us, our beautiful Earth, and our fellow travelers.

Working directly with the light is our next step. It doesn't cost us anything to see ourselves happier, more abundant, or full of joy. No one sends us a bill when we see our bodies in their ideal state of health. We don't need anyone's permission, and we don't have to be in a special place. Nor do we require the use of any fancy devices or tools. In fact, we don't need anything other than our imaginations and the light itself, and it's always there, just waiting for us to do with it as we please. It doesn't take long working with the light until we begin to shine brighter than ever.

When I was first learning to work consciously with light, it took a while for me to realize that, along with anything else I was envisioning, I could just as easily include myself, radiating complete and perfect joy, in the picture. This was a giant breakthrough and so, in an effort to enhance my light-working skills, I decided to ask Lee Ching if he had any pointers for me. Here's what he had to say:

*"Your joy walks with you every step of the way. You need look no further than that which is your own being. The world would have you think otherwise, and yet, what you do, how you think, and what you feel is entirely up to you. You are truly a magnificent entity with powers lying dormant and feelings so sublime, ready to*

*burst forth like a young flower that spreads its petals for the first time to greet the morning summer Sun.*

*How long will you wait before you see yourself in your highest light and do what makes you truly happy? What will it take for you to open your heart and radiate outward the ocean of Love that lies within you? You have been bound up too long, shackled to your fear, imprisoned by ghosts who are not real unless you make them so. The world needs you to be happy, to shine your light on all that you see, to laugh without limit, to touch the hearts and minds of every man, woman, and child who comes your way.*

*Take a chance now and live life as you've always wanted. Envision yourself throwing off the fetters of fear, and calling unto you the glory that is yours by right of birth. Let your joy blaze like a fire in the night. That's what the world needs from you.*

*And, more than that, that's what you need from yourself."*

The world we live in
is splitting apart.
The old selfish ways
are collapsing
and at the same time
the new spiritual ways
are emerging,
heralding a better life for all.
The old ways enslaved us.
The new ways free us.
The old ways were violent.

Shine Your Light

The new ways are nurturing.
The old ways kept us off balance,
on the run,
looking over our shoulders,
living in fear.

The new ways offer the promise of glory
where we shape the outcomes
of our experiences in advance,
where we have access
to all the energy and resources we need
to fulfill our life's purpose,
where we take our rightful place
within the perimeter
of a much bigger picture
that reaches out to us
as we reach out to it.

Those who are holding onto the old ways
at this time in history
are experiencing
ever-increasing states of discomfort.
Their rallying cries for violence
are being echoed back at them
until they hear the sobbing
from all the sorrow and suffering they create
and then choose to stand for peace instead.

Their profits amassed at the expense of others
are being charged back to them
until they experience
all the pain and poverty they create
and then choose to give and share instead.

Their schemes, which make use
of doubt and fear,
are being magnified and pointed back at them
until they see, ever so clearly,
all the darkness they create
and then choose to shine their lights instead.

It takes a measure of courage
to shine your light,
to stand up for what you know
in your heart of hearts
is true and good.
It asks you to align yourself
with something greater
than your small, needy self
and call it forth
every day
until it is a part of you.
It asks that you look within
and discover
the swirling sources of power
hidden along your spine

Shine Your Light

and connect them together
until a light comes on.
Breathe into it
and it will glow
and take you into parts of yourself
that lay dormant
yet have long awaited your call.

Now you can begin to explore
other places,
other possibilities,
other realms.

As your adventurous Spirit
pioneers into uncharted territories within,
it will open wide the gates
not only for you
but for others to follow.
You help your brothers and sisters
more than you know
as you shine your light
for all the world to see.

*Now you're ready to express yourself joyfully!* **The next time**
*you're in a group of people, and you're feeling a little intimidated*
*or afraid to take part like everybody else, go ahead and risk it. Let*
*it all hang out! If they're going to sing, sing along with them, and*
*do your best to let go and sing from your heart. If they're dancing,*
*join in and soon you'll discover that you're having so much fun you*

never want it to stop. If they're talking politics, speak your mind, but, for a change, take the conversation to a higher place, a place that suggests a positive outcome and advocates goodwill for all men and women.

From now on, be alert for any chance to come out of your shell. You'll be amazed at how good it feels after you've stepped out of the dark and begun to shine your light!

*The Light of God*
*shines into your heart*
*and quickens your step toward*
*that which will be.*
*Only you can recognize*
*the moment of its birthing.*

# THE NINTH INTENT
# SHARE YOUR VISION

*I create my ideal world by envisioning it and telling
others about it. I share my vision.*

If we truly desire to create a better world for ourselves,
we need to do something different than what we've been
doing. We need to think different thoughts and talk about
different things. At present, our thoughts and words are
dominated by ideas that keep us separated from one another,
beliefs that we are limited, and outcomes that have little or
no value to us personally, or to humanity at large. It's as if we
have all the tools we need to create a paradise on Earth, and
yet, these tools sit idle while we remain confused about what
we really came here to do.

Fortunately, as we've seen from the stories in this book,
many of us are breaking free from our urge to conform to the
old ways of doing things, and we are bringing like-minded

others along with us. Soon, enough of us will be thinking and talking about that which truly serves us—*and we will create a better world*. But first, we need to take a look at what's keeping us from experiencing our highest calling.

Most of us know that change is the only constant in the Universe. It's the one thing we can count on, and yet, a great many people remain inflexible, tied to beliefs and Earthly attachments that prevent them from reaching their highest potential. For the most part, fear is what causes us to stay locked in our old ways. Fear separates us from all of the wonders that are, by right of birth, ours to enjoy.

When we approach others with new ideas, it's common to bump up against their fears, and it is then that we would do well to remember that our energy is precious to us. We must not waste it on fruitless endeavors. This is not to say that we should refrain from planting the seeds of greatness in our fellow travelers. However, when we meet with strong resistance, we are wise to walk away and wait until our friends are more receptive.

Make no mistake. The intention of all those who truly care about humanity is that we are paving the way so that every man, woman, and child who treads upon this Earth is lifted up into a golden age of manifestation. Not one soul is to be left behind, but, as the First Intent states, we must allow others to have their own experiences, without our interference. If others choose to cling to their Earthly illusions, we must not push them. Instead, we can hold the light for them and trust that

Divine Grace will step in when the time is right. It is our job to remain steadfast in the knowledge that, once enough of us have overcome the mainstream inertia and lifted ourselves up, an ancient doorway will open for the entire body of humanity to pass through. In the meantime, we can use our energy wisely by spending it with those who are like-minded.

## – An Intenders Story –

*I'd like to share a story with you that happened to me recently. I'd been using the Intention Process for several years and was having great success with it until I moved into a new neighborhood. Almost from the day I moved in, everything went sour for me. The bills, which had never been a problem for me before, began to mount up, and, at the same time, my income took a drastic turn for the worse. I didn't know what to do. I was making my intentions every morning, but they'd stopped working for me. I was just about to give up on my intending when I ran across a piece of valuable information that turned everything around.*

*The information that helped me came in the form of a dream. In the dream, I was sitting under a large shade tree in a beautiful meadow with a wise man sitting before me. He was explaining that, if I wanted my intentions to manifest with less effort, I should not tell anyone else about them unless I was sure they were supportive of me and my work. He went on to say that other people can disrupt the manifestation of our intentions with their opposing thoughts, and that I needed to learn to discern between those who were in* alignment with me and the Highest Good and those who weren't. He said that, until I became more powerful in my own right, others could sabotage my intentions in ways that I'm not aware of.

Fortunately, the dream was so vivid that, when I woke up, I was still able to remember most of it. As I was writing it down in my journal, I realized that the wise man's words brought to light the exact situation I'd been experiencing in real life. When I moved into the new neighborhood, I'd become acquainted with a small group of people who seemed friendly at first, but who didn't really have my best interests at heart. They were a negative bunch who didn't like it when someone else enjoyed the success that they didn't have. Not only that, but when I explained the Intention Process to them, they were completely unaccepting of my ideas. In my efforts to clarify things for them, I even stated my intentions several times and mentioned the Highest Good, but it was obvious by the looks on their faces that they weren't "on my team." In fact, looking back on it all, they really didn't like the idea of anyone else becoming more empowered than they were.

Previous to this, I'd been sharing my intentions with almost everyone I met. I knew that my friends in the Intenders Circle I'd been going to for the last three years were aligned with me and the Highest Good, but, admittedly, I was naive about the motivations of others. As I began to look more closely into the motives of those around me, I realized that some people, even within my own family, had other plans for me. I needed to learn to be more careful with whom I shared my deepest desires.

As I write this, my bills are all paid up and my income is back to normal. Thanks to the wise man in my dream, I'm back on track

The Ninth Intent

*because, now, I'm more discerning. I only share my intentions with people who are on my team.*

Rick Borden
Dallas, TX

Perhaps, at this point, it would be a good idea to take a closer look at the wheels of inertia that keep the mainstream reality rolling along.

Inertia is the force that keeps something or someone in motion, and it also keeps something or someone at rest. In order to overcome it and have something new happen, a special kind of influence or energy is necessary. In terms of the quality of our lives, we have to care a lot more about our world than we've cared in the past. We need to start moving in a different direction. This is what *The Code* does, for embedded within its lines is the promise of a better life for all who are willing to think something new.

Let's take a look at an example to see how this works. If you sit in on the average casual conversation today, much of the talk would likely center around the national picture, what the politicians are doing, and where "we" are headed. You and your friends would probably agree that the national situation isn't giving you what you really want; that you seem to have lost your freedom, your peace, your own power to do with as you please; that our war-like tendencies simply aren't serving us anymore; that our distribution of goods and natural resources favors the "haves" and penalizes the bulk of the world's people; that you live in fear. You could go on and on listing the flaws in the current system, and almost everyone would have an opinion that would ostensibly help to make things better *from within the framework of the current system.* The current system, however, is first and foremost an illusion that *we choose to keep our attention on.* We could just as easily talk about something else if it weren't for the power of the inertia we keep bumping into. Just try to get your friends to set the topic of politics aside for a while, and see what happens. In most instances, it would be as if no one heard you. They'd keep on talking, lost in the inertia of the national collective mind.

There are those who would say that we're powerless to make changes in the face of collective inertia, but this simply isn't true. As we said earlier, changes occur when a new influence or energy is introduced into the picture. So let's shift the inertia by introducing The Code into our hypothetical scenario. We'll apply the Ninth Intent and make an intention around it by saying: *"I intend that I am creating my ideal world by envisioning it and telling others about it. I share my vision."* When we do this, our imaginations are unleashed. We have a new direction, one that gives us the autonomy to create our own vision, and the knowing that, in the envisioning, we are actively and consciously creating something better for ourselves. Our power instantly returns to us, and, from this point on, we're back on track, doing what we came here to do.

The hawks always appear
at the end of the day,
circling low over the fields.

In the same way,
the great messengers always arrive
at the end of an era,
circling with those who are ready
to hear the message
that a new day is here
and that their help is needed
to usher it in.

The season in which we live
is sweetened
for those who would do two things:
Once a day
envision and intend
that which we would create
and speak it aloud.
And once a week
gather with friends,
sit in a circle
and state our gratitudes and intentions
to the whole group.

When we begin to do this,
we move from passive to active,
from slumber to wakefulness,
from pawn to player.
And we engage
the Laws of the Universe

Share Your Vision

so powers unseen
will cocreate with us.

The Law is simple
and worth repeating.
Our thoughts and our words
are the building blocks
of our world.
Until recently,
we have not used this Law deliberately.
We have abdicated our place
on the throne of our own power,
allowing others to tell us
what to build,
how to live,
where to go,
and who to meet.

But now that a new day is here,
we are taking back
our place on the throne,
building a new world
from our own designs
with the knowledge that
we do have an effect,
we can make a difference,
and we are well prepared.

The Ninth Intent

If, on occasion,
you are bewildered
or lose your way,
know there is help
at all times,
in all places.
You can call upon
your angelic companions.
Invoke them
as often as you like.

Ask that they come
from 100 percent pure light,
the Light of Creation,
the Love of God,
and that the Highest Good
for all concerned
is served.

Ask them to guide,
to guard and protect you.
Bid them encircle
the fortress of your Being
so that inside
you are safe
and free
and at peace.

In this way,
you maintain a powerful environment
from which to expand your creation
and align with others
of light heart
and like mind
to bring about
an infusion of Love,
an awareness of Spirit,
and a way of life
to the peoples of Earth
so fulfilling,
so utterly and completely beautiful,
that you and all of your fellow travelers
are lifted up
and given to wander freely
in worlds of wonder
outside yourselves
and realms of rapture
within.

*The next time* *you find yourself grumbling about the way things are in the world, and you feel powerless to change any of it, take out a notebook and start writing about what your ideal world would look like to you. Describe, in detail, anything that comes to mind. You may choose to depict your ideal environment, the way you'd like people to act toward you, your perfect neighborhood, or your* ideal personal life. Write down the final outcome, not the steps it takes to get there. Leave those up to God.

Write as much as you feel like writing and then, when you've finished, take a mental snapshot of the visions you've written about and imprint each one indelibly in your mind.

And . . . **The next time** you're in the company of friends who are expressing their concern for the way things are going lately, instead of commiserating and feeling disempowered, share your mental snapshots with them. Do just as you'd do if you'd brought along your picture album from last summer's vacation. Point out all the little things they might miss, and, above all, tell them that their thoughts have the power to create a better world. Let them know that, when they're envisioning their ideal world and sharing it with others, they are bringing it to life.

*Create with Love*

*and your creation will Love you back.*

# THE TENTH INTENT
# SYNERGIZE

*I see Humanity as One. I enjoy gathering with light-hearted people regularly. When we come together, we set the stage for Great Oneness to reveal Itself. We Synergize.*

Now that we've formulated our vision of a better world and expanded it by sharing it with others, it's time to bring it into physical manifestation. To do this, we must come together. We must begin to make good use of the gifts that community has to offer.

In the dozen years that I've been taking part in Intenders Circles across the country, I've seen a lot of amazing things happen within the dynamics of a group. I've seen people who were introverted and frightened open up; I've seen my friends totally and utterly fulfilled; I've seen strangers recognize each other as members of a long-lost soul family; I've seen tears of joy flow and laughter abound. But there is one thing that happens in our Intenders Circles that, to me, is better than all the rest. It's what I call Synergy, and if we do things right, and set the stage properly, a very special feeling—a feeling of Oneness—will engulf the room and everyone in it. When this happens, it's as if we've completely let go of our connection to the cares and worries of the day and melted into something larger than ourselves. That's what Synergy is—it's what occurs when the whole becomes something greater than the sum of its individual parts. Put another way, it's when you put things together and "something extra" that you may not have expected takes place.

Examples of Synergy abound in Nature and perhaps one of the best is in how electricity is created. If you take a common iron bar and a ball of copper wire and you wrap the copper around the iron bar in a coil and give it a spin, all of a sudden, you have created electricity. You have created power. The bigger the bar of iron, the more copper you use, and the faster you spin it, the more power you will generate. But that's not the point. The point is that something has been created out of nothing. The electricity wasn't there before you brought the individual parts together, placed them in proper relation to each other, and then set them in motion.

What we found in our Intenders Circles is that people can do the same thing. We can set the stage for an experience of Synergy to occur by following the Oneness Formula. The Oneness Formula consists of six steps we go through after everyone has finished stating their gratitudes and intentions.

They are: (1) Sitting or standing together in a circle; (2) Touching; (3) Inviting; (4) Turning; (5) Toning; and (6) Holding the Silence. We've discovered that, when we follow these steps, the electricity, the magic, the Oneness, the special feeling that brings us closer to God usually happens. We have taken the adage, "Anywhere two or more are gathered in My Name (or for the Highest Good)," and put it to its best use. After all, isn't that what people are supposed to do when they gather together for spiritual purposes? Wouldn't it be wise for us to explore the highest of experiences available to us whenever we come together? These are some of the questions we sought to answer as we began to tap into the power of the Intenders Circle.

The first step in the Oneness Formula calls for us to arrange ourselves in a circle. In ancient times, most cultures knew to sit in a circle when they came together as a group. It was common sense to make it easy for everyone to have access to everyone else. Sitting in a circle, the group felt the power of something greater than its individual members. The connection with each other and with God was assured, and it enabled the people back then to perform great feats, build magnificent structures, accomplish seemingly unimaginable tasks, all because of the power created in the circle.

*I have memories of a time, tens of thousands of years ago, when we were much more powerful than we are now. Groups of eight of us (or sometimes sixteen) would go into caves especially designed for their symmetry and we would sit in a perfect circle with giant*

*crystals behind us that were connected to the crystalline benches*
*we sat on. We agreed beforehand on a few specific objects that we*
*intended to manifest, and then we would meditate and concentrate*
*our imaginations on those objects—and soon, sometimes instanta-*
*neously, they would materialize at a point in the exact center of the*
*circle, floating in midair, right in front of us.*

Somewhere along the way, as the great civilizations that pre-
ceded the one we're living in today began to degenerate, a few
powerful, avaricious people wanted to know what it would
be like to lord over everyone else. When that happened, the
power of the circle was forgotten and replaced by the podium/
audience arrangement. Now those who stood in front of the
group garnered the power unto themselves, and much of the
energy that was previously used to create Oneness among the
entire congregation was lost.

You see this arrangement still being used in most of our
churches today, and it is the reason why so many of them are
struggling. The people who attend church services do so in
order to get a true spiritual feeling—a feeling of Oneness—
but, most often, they leave the service without it. The reason
for this is because the churches have neglected to set the stage
for Oneness to occur. They spend their time with sermons,
solemn prayers, and singing hymns (to which few know the
words) but, other than that, they are too fear based and seem
to be in a hurry to get it all over with so the next service can
start on time.

I have attended services in many diverse religions and have rarely walked out of them with the lighthearted feeling I get at the end of an Intenders Circle. There are exceptions, of course. Many Unity, Religious Science, Unitarian Universalist, New Thought, Baha'i, and Gospel churches stand and hold hands in a big circle and sing together at the end of their services. These wonderful forward-thinking churches come the closest to creating a true spiritual environment for their parishioners; if only they would do a little more by putting the Oneness Formula to the test. Indeed, all the inspiring speeches in the world can't compare to a few moments of being bathed in the light of Oneness. *Achieving Oneness should be the highest priority for all who gather together for spiritual purposes.*

Once we've gathered in a circle, either sitting or standing, the next step is to touch each other. We do this by holding hands. Holding hands creates a connection between every-one in the room, just like you get when you string Christmas lights together around the tree. With some strands of lights, if one bulb is loose or burns out, it will keep the whole tree from lighting up. It is the same with people. If one person breaks the continuum by letting go of their neighbor's hand, there will be a subtle change in the energy in the room. The feeling of Oneness will tend to dissipate. I was in a circle in Portland, Oregon recently where about twenty of us were enrapt in a state of Oneness, and suddenly one man let go of the hand of the person beside him and it immediately brought the whole group back to their everyday perceptions. We could have stayed in that sacred state much longer if we hadn't broken the circle so quickly.

Of course, the feeling does linger after we "unplug" from each other. Indeed, once we've had a taste of the Synergy/Oneness Experience, we can learn to seek it out and sustain it as much as possible so that we become even more familiar with it. This is the antidote to all the separatist, us-versus-them, divide-and-conquer plots that have been put into place in our world. As we realize that our highest calling requires us to come together in order to create peace, freedom, and great works for ourselves, we understand that this is how it begins. It begins in small groups of people gathering in circles, holding hands with one another, and cultivating Oneness.

The next step is to call forth help from the invisible realms that surround us. There are many different ways of doing this and all of them work, as long as the Highest Good, Great Oneness, or God is invoked. Once we're formed into a circle and holding hands, one of us will express our gratitude, bless our time together, and then begin to call in our angels, guides, and helpers. He or she will usually say something like, "We invite and we invoke Jesus Christ, Buddha, Mother Mary, Mohammed, Kuan Yin, Yogananda, Lee Ching, the Ascended Masters, the Archangels, the dolphins and the whales, Chief Seattle, Ernest Holmes, the Nature Spirits, etc.," and then say, "Who else?" whereupon the people in the circle will also call in their favorite guides. When this is complete, the person who began the invitation will say, " . . . and we call forth all those who stand tall for the Highest Good, including all of

God's holiest angels, and we give great thanks that you join us here this evening. We ask that you help in bringing our intentions and visions into manifestation in great measure. And so be it and so it is!"

For those of you who have never done anything like this, we encourage you to check it out and see for yourself what it is like. Our experience has shown us that even the most analytical people who may have never fully explored the richness of their feelings will know that something special is going on once the invitation is underway. By taking part in an invitation like this, many have awakened to the power of their feelings. Indeed, in order to make contact with the higher spiritual realms, we must make friends with our feelings.

The next two steps are turning and toning. You can do either one, but doing both ensures that a state of Oneness will be reached. Turning is imagining that you are part of a wheel of light that begins to turn or spin on its axis. This is something we do with the remarkable light-working tool that we call our imagination. After the invitation is complete (and we have made the "holding the silence announcement," which I'll describe in a moment), we listen to one person lead us through a guided exercise that is specifically designed to bring on the Synergy/Oneness Experience. It involves us closing our eyes and letting go of everything except the vision that's being created in our minds.

Here is an example of a Synergy Exercise that we use quite often. There are more of these special exercises included at the end of this chapter, as well as on page 29 of *The Intenders*

*Handbook.* We also show you how to do a Synergy Exercise in *The Intenders* video. All of these exercises have been tested in our Intenders Circles and have been found to set the stage for us to easily step into a state of Oneness.

*"Everyone, please take three deep breaths, letting each one out with an 'Ahhh' sound . . . Now, close your eyes and imagine, if you will, a beautiful radiant light issuing from the center of your chest, from the center of your heart. Now, as you relax, notice that this wonderful light is spreading throughout your chest. It feels like a warm, soothing liquid, made out of God's holy, healing Love, expanding throughout your entire body, to the ends of your arms and legs, through your hands and feet. You feel radiantly alive and filled with Love for all living things. Now, imagine that this wonderful, healing light is extending out past the walls of your skin and overlapping with the light emanating from the people on each side of you, so that now you are a part of a circle or a wheel of light that's getting brighter and brighter.*

*"Now, imagine, if you will, that the wheel is beginning to spin or turn clockwise, and that its energy is passing through you, coming from right to left, moving from hand to hand. And now, the wheel begins to spin faster and as it picks up speed, it glows even brighter, and—as when you spin anything fast enough—it begins to make a sound. And the sound is 'Ahhh.' Everybody tone, 'Ahhh' . . ."*

From this point on, we're into the toning. Toning is, by far, one of the most powerful tools available to mankind. The purpose of toning is for each person to find his or her own voice, and then blend harmoniously with everyone else and become one voice. In other words, we tone as if we are singing a round, with each of us taking a fresh breath and continuing the tone immediately after we've run out of the last breath. We don't stop and wait for others to finish and start again; we keep it going.

We've also found that the longer it lasts, the better we feel. Most groups like to tone for three to five minutes, but I've been fortunate to tone in some circles that like to go on for ten to twenty minutes and, believe me, there are few feelings to compare with the experience of an extended toning.

The final step in the Oneness Formula is holding the silence. In our Intenders Circles, we've learned to hold the silence for a few moments after our toning in order to allow everyone to immerse themselves totally in the sacred feeling that's circulating throughout the room. In fact, it's a standard rule of thumb that we hold the silence for at least as long as we've toned. Holding the silence means that everyone remains still, even those who aren't very grounded. We have noticed in our Intenders Circles that the feeling of Oneness that we've worked to create has been spoiled on occasion by one or two people who feel so good that they can't help but let out a yell or a whoop. Or they'll let go of the hands of the people on each side, and they'll start fidgeting or talking. Our response to those who have a tendency to do this is: Please don't! Please respect everyone else and allow them to enjoy the fullness of the experience we've created for a few moments.

Recently, we've made it a policy, prior to beginning our Synergy Exercises that end our Intenders Circles, to announce for everyone to remain silent after the toning "so that the angels can work their magic." This announcement puts the ungrounded people on alert to keep quiet out of respect for others, and it also gives them an opportunity to become more uplifted than they would have if they had whooped or yelled.

## — An Intenders Story —

*We had a lady named Carol in the early days of The Intenders whom we liked very much, and yet Carol was so unaware of what others around her were experiencing that we had to take her aside one evening and clue her in to what she was doing. It seems that every time Carol got to feeling really good in our circle, she couldn't help but express herself loudly. Her noises usually came in the form of "Ooo's" and "Ahh's" but sometimes, when she felt especially good, she'd just blurt out, "I feel great!" or "Wow!"*

*Now, normally, this would be fine with the rest of us. However, when it happened at the end of our toning, we noticed that it interrupted the feeling of Oneness we were enjoying, and on those evenings we didn't go home feeling as good as we usually did. Later, when we talked about this situation and how to resolve it, we discovered that the Intenders Circle Format was subtly designed to build up to a particular feeling, and we had become accustomed to communing with Great Oneness at the end of the night. Carol's outbursts, although heartfelt and innocent, were affecting the rest of us to the point where we had to gently coach her on staying more anchored to the Earth and respecting what everyone else had come to the circle to experience. In Carol's case, she was so sweet and understanding that, from then on, not only did she hold the silence and allow the rest of us to have our sacred moments, she also began to mellow out and become more centered in herself.*

Tony Burroughs
Pagosa Springs, CO

The Intenders Circle Format can be used by anyone who wants to get together with their friends and neighbors and improve their lives. It creates a supportive environment where people can become empowered and build community at the same time. It has been tested over and over again by groups all across the globe and found to work no matter where you live, how many people you have, or whether you adapt it to suit your own needs. The Intenders are not proprietary; that is, we do not care what you call yourselves or if you combine parts of our format with other teachings that resonate with you. There are so many powerful and inspiring groups coming together at this time. In fact, we at The Intenders would like to acknowledge and applaud a few of them for the great light-work they are doing.

Many people are now gathering in CWG/Humanity's Team Sacred Circles to read from the *Conversations with God* books by Neale Donald Walsch and discuss these eye-opening principles. The CWG writings are truly changing the way we look at our world and causing us to reevaluate many of the old programmed beliefs that are no longer working for us. It is very common for Intenders to be familiar with the CWG writings and vice versa. In fact, several of the CWG groups around the country have been resourceful in combining their CWG readings and discussions with an Intenders Circle. They study the CWG material during the first hour of the evening and then have an Intenders Circle after that. And, of course, they have a Synergy exercise at the end of the meeting because it brightens the light of each person, and it increases the light in the entire neighborhood and beyond.

Other wonderful groups are discovering this as well. Many are meeting regularly to listen to the very inspiring Abraham/Hicks tapes; to read and discuss the *Course in Miracles*; to work for peace in James Twyman's Beloved Community; to share their feelings in Tej Steiner's Heart Circles; to watch *The Secret* or another great movie from the ever-expanding Spiritual Cinema collection; to join in a prayer circle at their local church, and afterwards, instead of socializing or going home right away, to take just a few moments to state intentions and Synergize by using the Oneness Formula.

Coming together and consciously imagining and spreading the light are the most important things we can do in these turbulent times. Whenever a group of any kind follows the Oneness Formula and consciously calls forth and extends the light in their area, the light remains there. That's why people like to have Intenders Circles in their home, because, on an invisible but very real level, the light stays and subtly touches all who live and visit there. We call upon all spiritual communities, churches, forward-thinking book, tape, and Spiritual Cinema clubs to begin to integrate an Intenders Circle into your meetings. There's no need to reinvent the wheel when it's already there for you. After your reading and discussion, prayer circle, or spiritual movie-watching, you can simply state your gratitudes and intentions into your circle, follow that with the Oneness Formula, and see what a difference it makes. You will feel lighter, happier, as if you've found a safe port out of the storm where you can now begin to consciously recreate your life and come into alignment with another larger, more expansive part of yourself.

You see, each one of us is like a cell in a gigantic entity that we call humanity. When we all work together synergistically, then all is well and we are capable of great things. Conversely, when we work against each other and humanity as a whole, each one of us suffers. The days of suffering, however, are coming to an end as every man, woman, and child begins to let go of the old ways that keep us apart from one another and embrace each other as One.

More and more of us are now realizing that the Being that resides in our bodies is the same Being or Spirit that resides in all bodies. We may be shaped differently on the outside, and have different experiences that have made us the way we are, but, inside, we are all the same. We are reaching the point in our evolution where we have done just about everything there is to do as individuals identified with our ego personalities, and now we are ready to do what we really came here to do. We are ready to come together for the Highest Good of All.

It sounds nearly impossible, given the current headlines and most peoples' tendency to go along with the mainstream, however an acceleration is upon us, and things are changing rapidly at this time. People everywhere are dropping their support for anyone who advocates violent solutions. We are getting rid of our weapons and withdrawing the sword of judgment that has been aimed at our fellow travelers. Time and time again, we have had seemingly dangerous situations threaten us, and we have learned to come together "en masse" and intend that the Highest Good for all of us is served. And with that intention, the Grace of God has repeatedly shown Itself and lifted our burdens.

Thus, we find ourselves nurturing a newfound trust in our fellow man. We are remembering how good it feels to live in a world where we are free to express ourselves as we like, with no thought of harm entering our lives. And we are consciously seeking out the highest potentials that are within us. Indeed, we are blossoming in all our glory. Peace, freedom, creativity, abundance, and joy for all are ours for the *intending*. Worlds within worlds reveal themselves as atom and galaxy alike welcome us and bid us explore to our heart's content. All that and more await, but first we must do one more thing before we set out for new horizons.

We must begin to join together in small groups, and then use our collective imagination to connect these groups to one another. When enough of us are embracing the vision of all groups everywhere, merging our lights and coming together as One, we will reawaken to that which we have already known—that this feeling of Oneness is our home, our place of comfort where we find our true selves—and take a breather before embarking upon other exciting adventures out there in the endless, eternal Universe.

People want peace.
People long to be free.
The only question is,
how do we get there?

We've been taught that we are free
because we live in America,
or Germany, or some other country
that was created with high ideals.
But does where we live really make us free?

We've been led to believe that we are free
because there is someone else out there
who is looking out for us,
or who is fighting for us,
or who died on a cross for us.
But has that really made us free?

Are we free to do as we please,
to create to our heart's content,
to walk this Earth innocently,
to talk to people about what we are creating
with our everyday thoughts and words?

The freedom that we have been sold
is not freedom at all.

Synergize

It is but a facade
built by those who would hide behind it
as they threaten to harm or kill
anyone who does not conform,
who does not pay the piper,
who seeks to rise above
their Earthly fears and debts
or looks to abandon their allegiance to those
who do not care one whit about them.

If we are to redefine our freedom
so that it serves us once again,
*we must come together.*
The answers are not to be found
in the solutions offered to us
by large institutions or corporations
that have a vested interest in their own greed,
that are willing to deceive for their own gain,
that are ready to kill to gratify their next whim.

The kind of freedom that these people offer
is not freedom at all.
It is not the kind of freedom
that humanity longs for.
The kind of freedom that we long for
does not require us to kill anyone,
to harm anyone,
or to judge anyone.

The Tenth Intent

The kind of freedom that humanity longs for
asks us to explore what we have in common
instead of our differences,
to cultivate our connectedness
instead of that which separates us.
It calls for us to come together as One
if we are to make a difference:
first, by gathering in small circles of friends
in neighborhoods and community centers,
in private homes and churches everywhere,
and then, by learning to Synergize.

For as we rediscover
how good it feels
to experience the joy of Oneness
within a small group,
we can then imagine how much better it will feel
when enough of us have come together
to create a shift
in the way we act toward each other
so that we are living in a world
where everyone honors and blesses everyone else,
where peace is taken for granted,
and where we are truly free
to express ourselves as we like.

Until now we have discounted
the profound effects

that a small group can have upon the world.
We've underestimated the power of the light
that a small gathering of people can generate
as they extend that light
out for as far as they can imagine.

The shift we long for
and the freedom and peace that accompany it
will come because enough small groups of people
will have come together
and used their imagination
to fill our world with light.

For just as our thoughts filter down
from the invisible to the visible,
so does the light we create
filter down into our world.

And one day soon,
our world will be so full of light
that the dark will be banished from here forever
and we will live in true peace
and true freedom.
Not the freedom that comes
from appeasing harsh masters,
but the freedom
that we find within ourselves
when we come together
for the Highest Good.

The Tenth Intent

*And so, **the next time** you're wondering about how to make your life better, why don't you get on the phone and start making arrangements to get together with a few of your friends for the purpose of socializing and, at the same time, setting the stage for an experience of Oneness to occur. It really doesn't matter how many people you're able to round up. There simply needs to be "two or more" of you. Nor does it matter how you proceed, just as long as you dedicate your time together to the Highest Good.*

*There are no particular rules for you to follow. The days of inflexible rules have come and gone. Some groups will prefer to plan community projects and some will like to listen to spiritual messengers or read their favorite books together. Others may choose to watch an uplifting movie, and still others may decide to meditate, pray, chant, drum, or sing songs together. These are all good ways for you to gather in community, and each will have a positive effect on all who attend.*

*Before you go home, however, we suggest that you arrange yourselves in a circle and, first, each state your gratitudes and intentions for your life and for your world, and then, finish the afternoon or evening off with a Synergy Exercise. Make your invitations, hold hands, call in the light, set it to spinning, and then tone any sound you like until a blending occurs. When you've finished, be sure to hold the silence long enough for the angels to work their magic.*

*When the silence is finally broken, you may find that you feel better than you've felt in years. Oftentimes you will feel so good that you'll just stand there, enrapt in the glow of Spirit. One thing is certain: you won't easily forget an experience like this. And all it* took was you letting your inhibitions go for a short time and being willing to go in search of the greatest thing that can happen wherever two or more people are gathered . . .

## Additional Synergy Exercises

*Close your eyes, take a deep breath or two, and relax, letting all the cares and worries of the day go for these few moments. Now, in your mind's eye, picture a beautiful angelic Being standing in the center of your circle. It may be Jesus Christ, Mother Mary, White Buffalo Calf Woman, Archangel Michael, Buddha, or whoever you choose. Imagine, however, that this wondrous Being is so tall that his or her head almost touches the ceiling of the room you're in, and also that, no matter where you are sitting, this heavenly Being is always facing you because he or she has the magical ability to face in all directions at the same time.*

*You see a wide, beautiful smile cross the face of this Being now, and even more than that, you feel the love in its heart for you and for all living things. And now you notice that the Being is raising its arm and pointing at the center of your chest, whereupon you feel a softening inside, and your heart opens up like never before. You feel this Being's love transferred into you in all its fullness, so that now you are experiencing what it is like to feel the Love that this angelic Being feels all of the time.*

*Let this Love settle and expand throughout your entire body and spread outward further in all directions for several feet so that it merges and blends with the Love from the person on each side of you. Imagine now, that you can see this Love in the form of sparkly,* energetic light that has now shaped itself into a circle that overlaps and blends into your circle of 3-D physicality. Now, take a deep breath and feel the circle of light and Love begin to spin clockwise, moving through you from right to left, from hand to hand. And as it picks up speed and brightens, you blend into All That Is going on around you by making a sound. "Ahhh! . . ." Everybody tone, "Ahhh! . . ."

Take a few deep breaths and close your eyes. The circle is complete now and everyone is holding hands, so that we are all connected with one another. Now, each and every one of us can begin to fill ourselves with light, starting by imagining a beautiful glow of God's healing, loving light coming forth from our hearts and spreading gently, yet quickly throughout our bodies. When it has reached your extremities, act as if you have an internal rheostat (or dimmer switch) so that now you turn the dial and your light becomes brighter and brighter.

Now, name one person (Susie, for example), take a deep breath, fill yourself with light, and as you exhale, send your beautiful light and all the Love that's in it out to everyone else in the circle. Now, the next person (Margaret, for example), you do the same. Fill yourself up with light as you inhale, and then as you exhale, extend your light out to everyone else in the circle. Now, Matthew, it's your turn. Breathe in, and fill with light, send your light out to everyone else as you breathe out.

Now . . . everyone else—all at the same time—take a deep breath, fill yourself with light, and as you exhale, send your light out to everyone else in the circle, so that now we are all sending and receiving light from each other, creating a beautiful grid or cylinder of light in the room that elongates upward to the heavens and beneath us all the way into the heart of Mother Earth.

As this column of light becomes even brighter, you notice that it is beginning to spin slowly. You feel yourself being gently pulled upward within the column to a place above the Earth where you see other columns of light in the distance. They're getting brighter as well, and now they are expanding and beginning to connect with one another. As each one brightens, expands, and merges with those around it, an instantaneous flash of crystal-white light occurs and encompasses all and everything around you in a feeling of sublime Love. You feel exalted and at peace as you let go and slip into the Oneness of the Light.

*You serve yourself well
by getting people together
so that they can begin to help each other.
There are groups
that are scattered all around,
not knowing that the others even exist.
It is for you to help
in bringing them together*

The Tenth Intent

so that they know about each other

and each other's good works.

That way, you can help each other

when it comes time

to make those stronger stands

for things like peace, equality,

freedom, sharing,

and creating a pure,

pristine environment for yourselves.

# THE NINTH INTENT REVISITED

Since we began The Code Workshops, we've heard so many inspiring visions from people who have set the Ninth Intent that we decided to share some of them with you. The overall feeling we get from these visions is that the people who told them to us had awakened from their indifference, and were now more enlivened and empowered to make their world a better place in which to live. What excited us most was that these people frequently mentioned that they felt so empowered by what they were doing that they couldn't wait to get together with their friends and ask them the question: *If you were already living in your ideal world, when you look around, what do you see?*

As you will discover, some of these visions are profound. The icing on the cake comes from the fact that the people who set the Ninth Intent with us *knew* that when they were sharing their vision of an ideal world, they were actively contributing to the creation of it.

You will also see that we've left a space at the end of this book for you to jot down some visions of your own. If you'd like, you can even share your visions with the world by writing them on our Internet Intenders Circle at *www.intenders.com* forum in the section entitled The Ninth Intent.

Oh, and by the way . . . you needn't be concerned if the details of your visions are different than someone else's. It's the *intent* behind your vision that counts. Feel free to express yourself as you like, and *know* that when you set your intent for a better world, a better world will come to you.

*I see a world where the media and our politicians are being truthful with us, where they're no longer trying to sell us programs in disguise as something else. I see the media showing what's good in the world. I see everyone feeling supported, from the poorest person on the street to the richest person in the world; where nobody feels alone; everybody is as prosperous as they want to be; and each one of us has true free will to make our lives what we want them to be. I see clean air, clean water, and perfect health for every single person. I see us living in a world where we all cooperate with each other in supporting the fulfillment of whatever that person's dream is. I see a world where peace means peace, and everyone on Earth decides to choose peace, and to be at One with everyone else. I see a world where everyone sees God in everybody, and we all support the God-potential in each one of us. And I see a world where we* truly let the Source back onto planet Earth, where we're always laughing, where there's nothing but joy, and people are having a wonderful time in whatever they are doing, and where we're all allowed to be ourselves, no matter how silly that is.

Sean Allen

San Diego, CA

I see each and every one of us ascending . . . I see a world of brilliant color and abundance, and we're taking care of each other with love and compassion . . . I see a world where the political hierarchy chooses Oneness instead of separateness, and it is guided by the Highest Spiritual Good . . . where humanity and each flower, each tree, each dog and cat feels a connectedness, and it is like going back to an earlier time when we were all connected with Nature. I see a world where the diversity of Love that we experience in groups like this, with people that we don't know, [creates in us] a heartfelt spiritual connection, and it is felt walking down the street with each person we come in contact with. I envision the young people and the older people gathering in a "Love Station" where the older people come and take care of the youth or those who are sick, so there is a unity and a sense of community . . . I see a world where healing is not a matter of medicine anymore, but of light and touching; where people are really connected, both on a Spirit level and on a heart and soul level; where we're not afraid to expose our vulnerabilities so that our true essence comes out, and it is accepted, and it is growth oriented. And I see a world where we really take time to just be, and love, and grow. And if there are religious differences, that there is an acceptance, and we know that it's all God and it's *all Spirit . . . I see the skies open up and that which we did not know is now known to us so that our fear dissipates and Love takes its place.*

Julie Jensen
Point Loma, CA

*There is no reason, whatsoever, why every human being who walks this Earth couldn't be given everything that he or she needs. Scarcity, in all of its insidious forms, is tucked neatly away into our past and replaced by abundance beyond measure. Oppression gives way to a life of total freedom such as we have never before experienced. And fear is now seen for what it truly is—a cry in the dark for attention, a call for the gift of comfort and peace. For as that loving attention is freely given without reservation, a light so bright will shine forth on everyone and everything. The streets will be filled with people smiling at each other, wanting one and all to experience the joy that comes when we live our lives to the fullest. Everywhere you look there will be peace. We are cleansed of all impurity by the Living Universe as it surrounds us and bathes us in the Highest Light imaginable. Once again we are innocent as young babes, yet divinely empowered, and thrilled at the wonders that lie before us.*

excerpt from
The Highest Light Teachings
by Tony Burroughs

*I see us living in a world where the ego has gradually come to know us as the Master; where it goes on hold for periods of time because* the Master is really home, here in this moment. When the Master is home, whatever needs to be decided will be known in the moment it needs to be known, and any choice or decision will be in harmony with All That Is. There will be no need for rules and regulations because we'll exist here in the moment of Now where no living thing would ever hurt another living thing, and no person would ever abuse another person.

Rachmat Martin
Soquel, CA

I see spiritual communities being established all over the Earth. We're all joining together, and all of us are offering our talents to help each other with whatever is needed in any moment for the highest purpose. We're all in total Love and total joy, and we all feel really good . . . and, included with this, the Earth is moving to a higher realm, to the next dimension, so that our environment is being cleaned up, and all of the plants and animals that have disappeared will reappear. It's beautiful!

Bob Caprio
St. Augustine, FL

I see a world where we know, as children, what our life's paths are, and where our educational systems sustain that and teach us what we need to know for our life's purpose so we can do what we came here to do. I see a world where we're all safe, and we have community, and we're all enjoying our lives to the fullest.

Janene Roberts
San Diego, CA

*I envision the world as a gigantic playground where all of us human inhabitants experience collectively and connectively the thrill, joy, playfulness, and power of becoming like children again.*

*Karen Dowers*
*Bayfield, CO*

My understanding of this transitional period, going from the current date of 2004 into 2012, is that, although we're unaware of it, we are, right now, in a situation of multilayered Universes of Possibility, and we have been programmed to have a group consensus reality of a world within the frequency range that is designed and gated and fenced in by those controlling this Earth planet at this time. However, we have never been true prisoners of that frequency range, we've only been in compliance with this frequency containment. So, as we unfold into our awareness of Self as Creator, and as we come back and merge into the Universal Oneness of All That Is, we realize that we are existing everywhere at all points and, therefore, we also become aware that this Earth and its shift exists as a new possibility at a new frequency based upon our choices.

So, therefore, in this period leading up to 2012, for every choice we make, we shift frequency into a new world, a new Earth. I do not see a dramatic, sudden physical shift, but more that those awarenesses who have allowed themselves to be like sheep will go into a world that may experience cataclysms and physical changes as part of its natural recycling process and as part of its returning into the Mother. However, those of us who do not have the need to act out that drama, and, instead, understand ourselves as creator gods and goddesses, will move easily and effortlessly into an expanded reality of Earth and its predicted thousand years of peace and thousand years of Golden Age in a frequency pattern that is moment by moment by moment. So, as far as we do this—create our chosen reality as heaven-on-earth—moment by moment, we are creating a new world which, for the time being, is in synchronicity with the old world that is decaying. By 2012, the separation of these two Universes, these two realms, will be completed. And so [what we are experiencing in this time of transition] is merely a stepping across the bridge, a stepping up into an expanded reality that is Love based, and we will never experience the types of harsh changes or suffering as predicted by the Hopi Elder Prophecies, which will be the lot of those who, as they put it, "cling to the shore" that is fear based. But, instead, as we move into the center of the river, and realize that we are living in a fluid external reality based upon our thoughts and beliefs, we are free at any moment to create a world where we experience none of these cataclysmic things. And there will be those in that world who look back upon the prophecies and say, "How strange, they never came to pass."

But in parallel worlds, they did come to pass.

Kyra Kelm
Playa Del Rey, CA


I visualize the world as it was in the beginning, as it was created, where we walked with God, and we walked with the goddesses and all the gods and all the energies of light; where we know the healing of Oneness and what it is to be caring of Self and respective of Self, knowing that we're each created in the image of God—Father Mother God—and that we're here to bring Love to this Earth planet . . .

*that we're recognizing our path and are empowered within our-*
*selves in creating Heaven on Earth . . . that we're here to recognize*
*the gift in each other as we are allowing others to see and accept*
*and support us in our gifts . . . that we are recognizing the power*
*of thought and intention, and that we are each responsible for what*
*we create . . . that we remember that wherever we visualize, that's*
*where our thought will carry us; that we can transmigrate and tele-*
*port; and that we can be wherever we will to be and know that we*
*can create that for others also, if they wish it. I see all children filled*
*with light and feeling peaceful. I see a world where disharmony is*
*vanquished, and we all accept unconditional Love for ourselves.*

*Reverend Debra Feldman*
*North Park, CA*

*I see other worlds opening before us where we literally fly, where*
*we meet face to face with our loving guides and angels and helpers.*
*And we experience that which is called Oneness, and the Hand of*
*God touches the hearts of every man and woman on this Earth.*

*Tim Sullivan*
*St. Paul, MN*

*My vision is of a world where everyone is as happy as Rob and me;*
*where everyone has a home and loving companionship and all of*
*the things that they need freely given to them. I see a world where*
*our leaders are truly caring about us; where the TV and newspa-*
*pers are filled with fun, uplifting stories; and where the people of*
*the Earth have learned to set their intent only on behalf of causes*
*that benefit all of us.*

Epilogue

*I see a world that is healed, where all men and women have found their niche in life, just as Rob and I have. After recently leaving our jobs in the city, we went in search of a community of people who were dedicated to the growth of their inner potentials and the stewardship of the Earth—and what we found amazed us! We discovered groups of people who were actually cleansing and purifying ponds, lakes, rivers, and even parts of the ocean by touching their hands to the water and praying. We found communities who were growing the lushest gardens and feeding whole neighborhoods with delicious, healthy foods. We met with technologically based groups who were inventing all sorts of new devices designed to further our evolution. We even ran across sports communities filled with those who were putting their warrior tendencies to positive use. They were creating new games and forms of entertainment that were changing the way we look at recreation.*

*The community we liked the most (and the one we finally settled in) is very unique. They call it a Conscious Choral Community and, when I envision a better world, I see communities like this popping up everywhere. Our community works with sound, and we get together and harmonize our voices by singing or chanting or making tones. We never know where the sound is going to take us, but we are sure of one thing: the sound is healing.*

*Although we meet with our fellow community members every day to make our sounds, at least once a week we go to a place where people need help and we "harmonize" it. Last week, we went to a metropolitan hospital where hundreds of us walked around the entire building singing our healing tones, and guess what happened? Within three hours, every sick and injured patient in the whole place got up and walked out happy, healed, rejuvenated, and full of life!*

*I can only tell you that when you see something wonderful like this happen, it changes you forever. For Rob and myself, we know, when we're coming together in unity with our friends and making these beautiful sounds, that we're healing ourselves and those around us. We feel more alive, empowered, and expanded. Personally, after a choral harmonizing, I'm ready for anything! I can't wait for us to encircle shopping malls, businesses, schools, and even governmental structures and see the people inside lifted up, becoming better stewards of their surroundings, and more at peace within themselves.*

*Ultimately, I see enough people lined up within their individual communities, and then these communities all coming together for the Highest Good until we "harmonize" and heal our whole world. The Reunion, or critical mass, that the Intenders Tribe taught us about, is well underway now, but that's another story—one that Rob will want to tell you about.*

*Trish McCoy*
*Brighton, VA*

Now it's time for you to create your own vision. But before you do, it might help to take a deep breath and imagine for a few moments that everything you see around you is made out of light, and that you can have a direct effect on your world by using your imagination. Now breathe deeper, and let go even more. Let go of any immediate cares for your survival needs; let go and feel your true joy settle in as all of your

Earthly cares and concerns disappear. This is where you find your safe haven. This is where you are free to create to your heart's content.

Now that you're relaxed, you can prepare to formulate your vision of a better world. Know that everything you need is here for you. All sounds are within you. All sights are within you. All thoughts and feelings are within you. All That Is is within you, and all you have to do is close your eyes and let God show you how beautiful your new world can be . . .

*And, when you're ready,*
*you can share your vision here.*

*I see a world where . . .* _____

_____

_____

_____

_____

_____

_____

_____

# The Intenders of the Highest Good

I f you're seeking to be part of a community of like-minded and lighthearted people who are becoming empowered and lined up with the Highest Good at the same time, The Intenders is open to everyone. You can visit our Web site at *www.intenders.com/directory* to see if there is an Intenders Circle already in your area. Or if you would like to start your own circle, our Create Your Own Community Package will make it easy for you.

To contact us:
Visit: *www.intenders.com*
Email: office@intenders.com
Phone: 888-422-2420

If you have any questions about the fine points of intention-making, feel free to post them on our Web site forum at *www.intenders.com/forum* so that the entire Intenders community can help you. We also highly recommend The Intenders Bridge, our uplifting daily email message program, which is available free at *www.intenders.org*.

You can download a free 8.5 x 11 copy of *The Code* at *www.intenders.com/TheCode*.

# Remember

That which is meant to be yours will come to you. Just as those of you who are aligned with the Highest Good will eventually experience your highest ideal, so shall your daily needs be met. You need never worry about your survival, because there was a special mechanism put into place long ago that regulates and guarantees that everything you need will be there for you in the exact moment that you need it. Oftentimes it will not appear until the instant before it is needed, but you may be assured that while you are waiting you are being strengthened. As you learn to trust in this wondrous process, the obstacles and hardships of life fall by the wayside and are replaced by a serenity that knows no limit.

These times of great upheaval are truly gifts unto you. You are constantly surrounded by an environment that is conducive to bringing out your most fulfilling form of expression. Your ego, the part of you that is in service to yourself, is giving way to a much *larger, grander you—the you that is in service to others. You are blossoming in all your glory, and it is this blossoming that you have always longed for. Be open, be available, and, in the meantime, be at peace. Your prayers and intentions are all being answered.*

# About the Author

Tony Burroughs is a self-empowerment advocate and community maker whose work is defining the standard for the future. He has bridged the gap between the mainstream and the magical by cofounding The Intenders of the Highest Good, an intentional community dedicated to achieving the highest potential of the individual and  of the community. Tony was a gentleman farmer in Hawaii until a dozen years ago when he and three friends developed The Intention Process. This simple but practical empowerment technique successfully combines the Laws of Manifestation with an Intenders Circle so that people are able to express their intentions and gratitude and bring their desires into reality. He is the author of *The Intention Process* video and several books, including *The Intenders Handbook* and *The Highest Light Teachings*. Tony resides in Pagosa Springs, Colorado, and travels across North America giving workshops and working with fellow Intenders. Readers can learn more about Tony and Intender Circles at *www.intenders.com,* and by subscribing to The Intenders Bridge, a free, daily e-mail message.

# To Our Readers

Weiser Books, an imprint of Red Wheel/Weiser, publishes books across the entire spectrum of occult and esoteric subjects. Our mission is to publish quality books that will make a difference in people's lives without advocating any one particular path or field of study. We value the integrity, originality, and depth of knowledge of our authors.

Our readers are our most important resource, and we appreciate your input, suggestions, and ideas about what you would like to see published. Please feel free to contact us, to request our latest book catalog, or to be added to our mailing list.

Red Wheel/Weiser, LLC
500 Third Street, Suite 230
San Francisco, CA 94107
*www.redwheelweiser.com*